THIS LOG BOOK

NAME: _____

ADDRESS: _____

_____

PHONE NUMBER: _____

LOG BOOK DETAILS:

LOG START DATE: _____

LOG END DATE: _____

LOGBOOK NUMBER: _____

FISHING JOURNAL AND LOG BOOK

SPECIES BEING PURSUED _____

DATE: _____   TIME: _____   TO: _____

WHO I FISHED WITH: _____

WATER LOCATION DETAILS

BODY OF WATER: _____   LAUNCH RAMP: _____

WATER TEMP AT LAUNCH: _____   UPON RETURN : _____

WATER CLARITY:
☐ CLEAR ☐ STAINED ☐ MURKY ☐ MUDDY ☐ OTHER: _____

WATER LEVEL:
☐ NORMAL ☐ LOW ☐ HIGH ☐ DROPPING ☐ RISING

OTHER FACTORS:
☐ INSECT HATCHES ☐ BAIT FISH ☐ OTHER_____

WEATHER DETAILS

CURRENT AIR TEMP: _____   HIGH/LOW: _____/_____
WIND SPEED: _____   DIRECTION: _____
MOON PHASE: _____   BAROMETER: _____
SUNRISE: _____   SUNSET: _____

CONDITIONS NOTED:
☐ SUNNY ☐ PARTLY CLOUDY ☐ CLOUDY ☐ STORM CLOUDS
☐ RAINING ☐ FOG ☐ DRIZZLE ☐ SLEET ☐ SNOW
☐ OTHER: _____

NOTES: _____
_____
_____

SPECIES:_____ LENGTH:_____ WEIGHT:_____

TIME CAUGHT:_____ LOCATION:_____

STUCTURE/ VEGETATION: _____ DEPTH:_____
LURE / BAIT TYPE: _____

COLOR: _____ SIZE: _____ MODEL: _____

ROD: _____ REEL:_____ LINE: _____

NOTES: _____

_____

===

SPECIES:_____ LENGTH:_____ WEIGHT:_____

TIME CAUGHT:_____ LOCATION:_____

STUCTURE/ VEGETATION: _____ DEPTH:_____
LURE / BAIT TYPE: _____

COLOR: _____ SIZE: _____ MODEL: _____

ROD: _____ REEL:_____ LINE: _____

NOTES: _____

_____

===

SPECIES:_____ LENGTH:_____ WEIGHT:_____

TIME CAUGHT:_____ LOCATION:_____

STUCTURE/ VEGETATION: _____ DEPTH:_____
LURE / BAIT TYPE: _____

COLOR: _____ SIZE: _____ MODEL: _____

ROD: _____ REEL:_____ LINE: _____

NOTES: _____

_____

SPECIES:_____ LENGTH: _____ WEIGHT: _____

TIME CAUGHT:_____ LOCATION:_____

STUCTURE/ VEGETATION: _____ DEPTH: _____
LURE / BAIT TYPE: _____

COLOR: _____ SIZE: _____ MODEL: _____

ROD: _____ REEL:_____ LINE: _____

NOTES: _____

_____

SPECIES:_____ LENGTH: _____ WEIGHT: _____

TIME CAUGHT:_____ LOCATION:_____

STUCTURE/ VEGETATION: _____ DEPTH: _____
LURE / BAIT TYPE: _____

COLOR: _____ SIZE: _____ MODEL: _____

ROD: _____ REEL:_____ LINE: _____

NOTES: _____

_____

SPECIES:_____ LENGTH: _____ WEIGHT: _____

TIME CAUGHT:_____ LOCATION:_____

STUCTURE/ VEGETATION: _____ DEPTH: _____
LURE / BAIT TYPE: _____

COLOR: _____ SIZE: _____ MODEL: _____

ROD: _____ REEL:_____ LINE: _____

NOTES: _____

_____

SPECIES:_____ LENGTH:_____ WEIGHT:_____

TIME CAUGHT:_____ LOCATION:_____

STUCTURE/ VEGETATION: _____ DEPTH:_____

LURE / BAIT TYPE:
_____

COLOR: _____ SIZE: _____ MODEL: _____

ROD: _____ REEL:_____ LINE:_____

NOTES: _____

_____

═══════════════════════════════════════

SPECIES:_____ LENGTH:_____ WEIGHT:_____

TIME CAUGHT:_____ LOCATION:_____

STUCTURE/ VEGETATION: _____ DEPTH:_____

LURE / BAIT TYPE:
_____

COLOR: _____ SIZE: _____ MODEL: _____

ROD: _____ REEL:_____ LINE:_____

NOTES: _____

_____

═══════════════════════════════════════

SPECIES:_____ LENGTH:_____ WEIGHT:_____

TIME CAUGHT:_____ LOCATION:_____

STUCTURE/ VEGETATION: _____ DEPTH:_____

LURE / BAIT TYPE:
_____

COLOR: _____ SIZE: _____ MODEL: _____

ROD: _____ REEL:_____ LINE:_____

NOTES: _____

_____

SPECIES:_____ LENGTH:_____ WEIGHT:_____

TIME CAUGHT:_____ LOCATION:_____

STUCTURE/ VEGETATION: _____ DEPTH:_____
LURE / BAIT TYPE: _____

COLOR: _____ SIZE: _____ MODEL: _____

ROD: _____ REEL:_____ LINE:_____

NOTES: _____
_____

════════════════════════════════

SPECIES:_____ LENGTH:_____ WEIGHT:_____

TIME CAUGHT:_____ LOCATION:_____

STUCTURE/ VEGETATION: _____ DEPTH:_____
LURE / BAIT TYPE: _____

COLOR: _____ SIZE: _____ MODEL: _____

ROD: _____ REEL:_____ LINE:_____

NOTES: _____
_____

════════════════════════════════

SPECIES:_____ LENGTH:_____ WEIGHT:_____

TIME CAUGHT:_____ LOCATION:_____

STUCTURE/ VEGETATION: _____ DEPTH:_____
LURE / BAIT TYPE: _____

COLOR: _____ SIZE: _____ MODEL: _____

ROD: _____ REEL:_____ LINE:_____

NOTES: _____
_____

FISHING JOURNAL AND LOG BOOK

SPECIES BEING PURSUED _____

DATE: _____   TIME: _____   TO: _____

WHO I FISHED WITH: _____

WATER LOCATION DETAILS
BODY OF WATER: _____ LAUNCH RAMP: _____

WATER TEMP AT LAUNCH:_____ UPON RETURN : _____

WATER CLARITY:
☐ CLEAR ☐ STAINED ☐ MURKY ☐ MUDDY ☐ OTHER:_____

WATER LEVEL:
☐ NORMAL ☐ LOW ☐ HIGH ☐ DROPPING ☐ RISING

OTHER FACTORS:
☐ INSECT HATCHES ☐ BAIT FISH ☐ OTHER_____

WEATHER DETAILS
CURRENT AIR TEMP:_____ HIGH/LOW:_____/_____
WIND SPEED: _____ DIRECTION: _____
MOON PHASE: _____ BAROMETER:_____
SUNRISE: _____ SUNSET:_____

CONDITIONS NOTED:
☐ SUNNY ☐ PARTLY CLOUDY ☐ CLOUDY ☐ STORM CLOUDS
☐ RAINING ☐ FOG ☐ DRIZZLE ☐ SLEET ☐ SNOW
☐ OTHER: _____

NOTES: _____

_____

_____

SPECIES:_____ LENGTH:_____ WEIGHT:_____

TIME CAUGHT:_____ LOCATION:_____

STUCTURE/ VEGETATION: _____ DEPTH:_____
LURE / BAIT TYPE: _____

COLOR: _____ SIZE: _____ MODEL: _____

ROD: _____ REEL:_____ LINE: _____

NOTES: _____

_____

═══

SPECIES:_____ LENGTH:_____ WEIGHT:_____

TIME CAUGHT:_____ LOCATION:_____

STUCTURE/ VEGETATION: _____ DEPTH:_____
LURE / BAIT TYPE: _____

COLOR: _____ SIZE: _____ MODEL: _____

ROD: _____ REEL:_____ LINE: _____

NOTES: _____

_____

═══

SPECIES:_____ LENGTH:_____ WEIGHT:_____

TIME CAUGHT:_____ LOCATION:_____

STUCTURE/ VEGETATION: _____ DEPTH:_____
LURE / BAIT TYPE: _____

COLOR: _____ SIZE: _____ MODEL: _____

ROD: _____ REEL:_____ LINE: _____

NOTES: _____

_____

SPECIES:_____ LENGTH: _____ WEIGHT: _____

TIME CAUGHT:_____ LOCATION:_____

STUCTURE/ VEGETATION: _____ DEPTH: _____
LURE / BAIT TYPE: _____

COLOR: _____ SIZE: _____ MODEL: _____

ROD: _____ REEL:_____ LINE: _____

NOTES: _____
_____

SPECIES:_____ LENGTH: _____ WEIGHT: _____

TIME CAUGHT:_____ LOCATION:_____

STUCTURE/ VEGETATION: _____ DEPTH: _____
LURE / BAIT TYPE: _____

COLOR: _____ SIZE: _____ MODEL: _____

ROD: _____ REEL:_____ LINE: _____

NOTES: _____
_____

SPECIES:_____ LENGTH: _____ WEIGHT: _____

TIME CAUGHT:_____ LOCATION:_____

STUCTURE/ VEGETATION: _____ DEPTH: _____
LURE / BAIT TYPE: _____

COLOR: _____ SIZE: _____ MODEL: _____

ROD: _____ REEL:_____ LINE: _____

NOTES: _____

SPECIES:_____ LENGTH:_____ WEIGHT:_____

TIME CAUGHT:_____ LOCATION:_____

STUCTURE/ VEGETATION: _____ DEPTH:_____
LURE / BAIT TYPE:
_____

COLOR: _____ SIZE: _____ MODEL: _____

ROD: _____ REEL:_____ LINE: _____

NOTES: _____

_____

SPECIES:_____ LENGTH:_____ WEIGHT:_____

TIME CAUGHT:_____ LOCATION:_____

STUCTURE/ VEGETATION: _____ DEPTH:_____
LURE / BAIT TYPE:
_____

COLOR: _____ SIZE: _____ MODEL: _____

ROD: _____ REEL:_____ LINE: _____

NOTES: _____

_____

SPECIES:_____ LENGTH:_____ WEIGHT:_____

TIME CAUGHT:_____ LOCATION:_____

STUCTURE/ VEGETATION: _____ DEPTH:_____
LURE / BAIT TYPE:
_____

COLOR: _____ SIZE: _____ MODEL: _____

ROD: _____ REEL:_____ LINE: _____

NOTES: _____

_____

SPECIES:_____ LENGTH: _____ WEIGHT: _____

TIME CAUGHT:_____ LOCATION:_____

STUCTURE/ VEGETATION: _____ DEPTH: _____
LURE / BAIT TYPE: _____

COLOR: _____ SIZE: _____ MODEL: _____

ROD: _____ REEL:_____ LINE: _____

NOTES: _____

_____

SPECIES:_____ LENGTH: _____ WEIGHT: _____

TIME CAUGHT:_____ LOCATION:_____

STUCTURE/ VEGETATION: _____ DEPTH: _____
LURE / BAIT TYPE: _____

COLOR: _____ SIZE: _____ MODEL: _____

ROD: _____ REEL:_____ LINE: _____

NOTES: _____

_____

SPECIES:_____ LENGTH: _____ WEIGHT: _____

TIME CAUGHT:_____ LOCATION:_____

STUCTURE/ VEGETATION: _____ DEPTH: _____
LURE / BAIT TYPE: _____

COLOR: _____ SIZE: _____ MODEL: _____

ROD: _____ REEL:_____ LINE: _____

NOTES: _____

_____

FISHING JOURNAL AND LOG BOOK

SPECIES BEING PURSUED _____

DATE: _____ TIME: _____ TO: _____

WHO I FISHED WITH: _____

WATER LOCATION DETAILS

BODY OF WATER: _____ LAUNCH RAMP: _____

WATER TEMP AT LAUNCH: _____ UPON RETURN : _____

WATER CLARITY:
☐ CLEAR ☐ STAINED ☐ MURKY ☐ MUDDY ☐ OTHER: _____

WATER LEVEL:
☐ NORMAL ☐ LOW ☐ HIGH ☐ DROPPING ☐ RISING

OTHER FACTORS:
☐ INSECT HATCHES ☐ BAIT FISH ☐ OTHER_____

WEATHER DETAILS
CURRENT AIR TEMP: _____ HIGH/LOW: _____ / _____
WIND SPEED: _____ DIRECTION: _____
MOON PHASE: _____ BAROMETER: _____
SUNRISE: _____ SUNSET: _____

CONDITIONS NOTED:
☐ SUNNY ☐ PARTLY CLOUDY ☐ CLOUDY ☐ STORM CLOUDS
☐ RAINING ☐ FOG ☐ DRIZZLE ☐ SLEET ☐ SNOW
☐ OTHER: _____

NOTES: _____
_____
_____

SPECIES:_____ LENGTH:_____ WEIGHT:_____

TIME CAUGHT:_____ LOCATION:_____

STUCTURE/ VEGETATION:_____ DEPTH:_____
LURE / BAIT TYPE:
_____

COLOR:_____ SIZE:_____ MODEL:_____

ROD:_____ REEL:_____ LINE:_____

NOTES:_____
_____

SPECIES:_____ LENGTH:_____ WEIGHT:_____

TIME CAUGHT:_____ LOCATION:_____

STUCTURE/ VEGETATION:_____ DEPTH:_____
LURE / BAIT TYPE:
_____

COLOR:_____ SIZE:_____ MODEL:_____

ROD:_____ REEL:_____ LINE:_____

NOTES:_____
_____

SPECIES:_____ LENGTH:_____ WEIGHT:_____

TIME CAUGHT:_____ LOCATION:_____

STUCTURE/ VEGETATION:_____ DEPTH:_____
LURE / BAIT TYPE:
_____

COLOR:_____ SIZE:_____ MODEL:_____

ROD:_____ REEL:_____ LINE:_____

NOTES:_____
_____

SPECIES:_____ LENGTH: _____ WEIGHT: _____

TIME CAUGHT:_____ LOCATION:_____

STUCTURE/ VEGETATION: _____ DEPTH: _____
LURE / BAIT TYPE: _____

COLOR: _____ SIZE: _____ MODEL: _____

ROD: _____ REEL:_____ LINE: _____

NOTES: _____

_____

SPECIES:_____ LENGTH: _____ WEIGHT: _____

TIME CAUGHT:_____ LOCATION:_____

STUCTURE/ VEGETATION: _____ DEPTH: _____
LURE / BAIT TYPE: _____

COLOR: _____ SIZE: _____ MODEL: _____

ROD: _____ REEL:_____ LINE: _____

NOTES: _____

_____

SPECIES:_____ LENGTH: _____ WEIGHT: _____

TIME CAUGHT:_____ LOCATION:_____

STUCTURE/ VEGETATION: _____ DEPTH: _____
LURE / BAIT TYPE: _____

COLOR: _____ SIZE: _____ MODEL: _____

ROD: _____ REEL:_____ LINE: _____

NOTES: _____

_____

SPECIES:_____ LENGTH:_____ WEIGHT: _____

TIME CAUGHT:_____ LOCATION:_____

STUCTURE/ VEGETATION: _____ DEPTH: _____
LURE / BAIT TYPE: _____

COLOR: _____ SIZE: _____ MODEL: _____

ROD: _____ REEL:_____ LINE: _____

NOTES: _____

_____

SPECIES:_____ LENGTH:_____ WEIGHT: _____

TIME CAUGHT:_____ LOCATION:_____

STUCTURE/ VEGETATION: _____ DEPTH: _____
LURE / BAIT TYPE: _____

COLOR: _____ SIZE: _____ MODEL: _____

ROD: _____ REEL:_____ LINE: _____

NOTES: _____

_____

SPECIES:_____ LENGTH:_____ WEIGHT: _____

TIME CAUGHT:_____ LOCATION:_____

STUCTURE/ VEGETATION: _____ DEPTH: _____
LURE / BAIT TYPE: _____

COLOR: _____ SIZE: _____ MODEL: _____

ROD: _____ REEL:_____ LINE: _____

NOTES: _____

_____

SPECIES:_____ LENGTH:_____ WEIGHT:_____

TIME CAUGHT:_____ LOCATION:_____

STUCTURE/ VEGETATION:_____ DEPTH:_____

LURE / BAIT TYPE:_____

COLOR:_____ SIZE:_____ MODEL:_____

ROD:_____ REEL:_____ LINE:_____

NOTES:_____

_____

SPECIES:_____ LENGTH:_____ WEIGHT:_____

TIME CAUGHT:_____ LOCATION:_____

STUCTURE/ VEGETATION:_____ DEPTH:_____

LURE / BAIT TYPE:_____

COLOR:_____ SIZE:_____ MODEL:_____

ROD:_____ REEL:_____ LINE:_____

NOTES:_____

_____

SPECIES:_____ LENGTH:_____ WEIGHT:_____

TIME CAUGHT:_____ LOCATION:_____

STUCTURE/ VEGETATION:_____ DEPTH:_____

LURE / BAIT TYPE:_____

COLOR:_____ SIZE:_____ MODEL:_____

ROD:_____ REEL:_____ LINE:_____

NOTES:_____

_____

FISHING JOURNAL AND LOG BOOK

SPECIES BEING PURSUED _____

DATE: _____ TIME: _____ TO: _____

WHO I FISHED WITH: _____

WATER LOCATION DETAILS

BODY OF WATER: _____ LAUNCH RAMP: _____

WATER TEMP AT LAUNCH: _____ UPON RETURN : _____

WATER CLARITY:
☐ CLEAR ☐ STAINED ☐ MURKY ☐ MUDDY ☐ OTHER: _____

WATER LEVEL:
☐ NORMAL ☐ LOW ☐ HIGH ☐ DROPPING ☐ RISING

OTHER FACTORS:
☐ INSECT HATCHES ☐ BAIT FISH ☐ OTHER _____

WEATHER DETAILS

CURRENT AIR TEMP: _____ HIGH/LOW: _____ / _____

WIND SPEED: _____ DIRECTION: _____

MOON PHASE: _____ BAROMETER: _____

SUNRISE: _____ SUNSET: _____

CONDITIONS NOTED:
☐ SUNNY ☐ PARTLY CLOUDY ☐ CLOUDY ☐ STORM CLOUDS
☐ RAINING ☐ FOG ☐ DRIZZLE ☐ SLEET ☐ SNOW
☐ OTHER: _____

NOTES: _____

_____

_____

SPECIES:_____ LENGTH:_____ WEIGHT: _____

TIME CAUGHT:_____ LOCATION:_____

STUCTURE/ VEGETATION: _____ DEPTH: _____
LURE / BAIT TYPE: _____

COLOR: _____ SIZE: _____ MODEL: _____

ROD: _____ REEL:_____ LINE: _____

NOTES: _____

_____

SPECIES:_____ LENGTH:_____ WEIGHT: _____

TIME CAUGHT:_____ LOCATION:_____

STUCTURE/ VEGETATION: _____ DEPTH: _____
LURE / BAIT TYPE: _____

COLOR: _____ SIZE: _____ MODEL: _____

ROD: _____ REEL:_____ LINE: _____

NOTES: _____

_____

SPECIES:_____ LENGTH:_____ WEIGHT: _____

TIME CAUGHT:_____ LOCATION:_____

STUCTURE/ VEGETATION: _____ DEPTH: _____
LURE / BAIT TYPE: _____

COLOR: _____ SIZE: _____ MODEL: _____

ROD: _____ REEL:_____ LINE: _____

NOTES: _____

_____

SPECIES:_____ LENGTH:_____ WEIGHT:_____

TIME CAUGHT:_____ LOCATION:_____

STUCTURE/ VEGETATION: _____ DEPTH:_____
LURE / BAIT TYPE: _____

COLOR: _____ SIZE: _____ MODEL: _____

ROD: _____ REEL:_____ LINE: _____

NOTES: _____

_____

═══════════════════════════════════════

SPECIES:_____ LENGTH:_____ WEIGHT:_____

TIME CAUGHT:_____ LOCATION:_____

STUCTURE/ VEGETATION: _____ DEPTH:_____
LURE / BAIT TYPE: _____

COLOR: _____ SIZE: _____ MODEL: _____

ROD: _____ REEL:_____ LINE: _____

NOTES: _____

_____

═══════════════════════════════════════

SPECIES:_____ LENGTH:_____ WEIGHT:_____

TIME CAUGHT:_____ LOCATION:_____

STUCTURE/ VEGETATION: _____ DEPTH:_____
LURE / BAIT TYPE: _____

COLOR: _____ SIZE: _____ MODEL: _____

ROD: _____ REEL:_____ LINE: _____

NOTES: _____

_____

SPECIES:_____ LENGTH:_____ WEIGHT:_____

TIME CAUGHT:_____ LOCATION:_____

STUCTURE/ VEGETATION: _____ DEPTH:_____
LURE / BAIT TYPE: _____

COLOR: _____ SIZE: _____ MODEL: _____

ROD: _____ REEL:_____ LINE: _____

NOTES: _____

_____

SPECIES:_____ LENGTH:_____ WEIGHT:_____

TIME CAUGHT:_____ LOCATION:_____

STUCTURE/ VEGETATION: _____ DEPTH:_____
LURE / BAIT TYPE: _____

COLOR: _____ SIZE: _____ MODEL: _____

ROD: _____ REEL:_____ LINE: _____

NOTES: _____

_____

SPECIES:_____ LENGTH:_____ WEIGHT:_____

TIME CAUGHT:_____ LOCATION:_____

STUCTURE/ VEGETATION: _____ DEPTH:_____
LURE / BAIT TYPE: _____

COLOR: _____ SIZE: _____ MODEL: _____

ROD: _____ REEL:_____ LINE: _____

NOTES: _____

_____

SPECIES:_____ LENGTH:_____ WEIGHT:_____

TIME CAUGHT:_____ LOCATION:_____

STUCTURE/ VEGETATION: _____ DEPTH:_____
LURE / BAIT TYPE: _____

COLOR: _____ SIZE: _____ MODEL: _____

ROD: _____ REEL:_____ LINE: _____

NOTES: _____

_____

SPECIES:_____ LENGTH:_____ WEIGHT:_____

TIME CAUGHT:_____ LOCATION:_____

STUCTURE/ VEGETATION: _____ DEPTH:_____
LURE / BAIT TYPE: _____

COLOR: _____ SIZE: _____ MODEL: _____

ROD: _____ REEL:_____ LINE: _____

NOTES: _____

_____

SPECIES:_____ LENGTH:_____ WEIGHT:_____

TIME CAUGHT:_____ LOCATION:_____

STUCTURE/ VEGETATION: _____ DEPTH:_____
LURE / BAIT TYPE: _____

COLOR: _____ SIZE: _____ MODEL: _____

ROD: _____ REEL:_____ LINE: _____

NOTES: _____

_____

FISHING JOURNAL AND LOG BOOK

SPECIES BEING PURSUED _____

DATE: _____ TIME: _____ TO: _____

WHO I FISHED WITH: _____

WATER LOCATION DETAILS
BODY OF WATER: _____ LAUNCH RAMP: _____

WATER TEMP AT LAUNCH: _____ UPON RETURN : _____

WATER CLARITY:
☐ CLEAR ☐ STAINED ☐ MURKY ☐ MUDDY ☐ OTHER: _____

WATER LEVEL:
☐ NORMAL ☐ LOW ☐ HIGH ☐ DROPPING ☐ RISING

OTHER FACTORS:
☐ INSECT HATCHES ☐ BAIT FISH ☐ OTHER_____

WEATHER DETAILS
CURRENT AIR TEMP: _____ HIGH/LOW: _____ / _____
WIND SPEED: _____ DIRECTION: _____
MOON PHASE: _____ BAROMETER: _____
SUNRISE: _____ SUNSET: _____

CONDITIONS NOTED:
☐ SUNNY ☐ PARTLY CLOUDY ☐ CLOUDY ☐ STORM CLOUDS
☐ RAINING ☐ FOG ☐ DRIZZLE ☐ SLEET ☐ SNOW
☐ OTHER: _____

NOTES: _____
_____
_____

SPECIES:_____ LENGTH:_____ WEIGHT:_____

TIME CAUGHT:_____ LOCATION:_____

STUCTURE/ VEGETATION: _____ DEPTH:_____

LURE / BAIT TYPE: _____

COLOR: _____ SIZE: _____ MODEL: _____

ROD: _____ REEL:_____ LINE: _____

NOTES: _____

_____

═══════════════════════════════════════

SPECIES:_____ LENGTH:_____ WEIGHT:_____

TIME CAUGHT:_____ LOCATION:_____

STUCTURE/ VEGETATION: _____ DEPTH:_____

LURE / BAIT TYPE: _____

COLOR: _____ SIZE: _____ MODEL: _____

ROD: _____ REEL:_____ LINE: _____

NOTES: _____

_____

═══════════════════════════════════════

SPECIES:_____ LENGTH:_____ WEIGHT:_____

TIME CAUGHT:_____ LOCATION:_____

STUCTURE/ VEGETATION: _____ DEPTH:_____

LURE / BAIT TYPE: _____

COLOR: _____ SIZE: _____ MODEL: _____

ROD: _____ REEL:_____ LINE: _____

NOTES: _____

_____

SPECIES:_____ LENGTH:_____ WEIGHT:_____

TIME CAUGHT:_____ LOCATION:_____

STUCTURE/ VEGETATION:_____ DEPTH:_____
LURE / BAIT TYPE:_____

COLOR:_____ SIZE:_____ MODEL:_____

ROD:_____ REEL:_____ LINE:_____

NOTES:_____

_____

SPECIES:_____ LENGTH:_____ WEIGHT:_____

TIME CAUGHT:_____ LOCATION:_____

STUCTURE/ VEGETATION:_____ DEPTH:_____
LURE / BAIT TYPE:_____

COLOR:_____ SIZE:_____ MODEL:_____

ROD:_____ REEL:_____ LINE:_____

NOTES:_____

_____

SPECIES:_____ LENGTH:_____ WEIGHT:_____

TIME CAUGHT:_____ LOCATION:_____

STUCTURE/ VEGETATION:_____ DEPTH:_____
LURE / BAIT TYPE:_____

COLOR:_____ SIZE:_____ MODEL:_____

ROD:_____ REEL:_____ LINE:_____

NOTES:_____

_____

SPECIES:_____ LENGTH: _____ WEIGHT: _____

TIME CAUGHT:_____ LOCATION:_____

STUCTURE/ VEGETATION: _____ DEPTH: _____
LURE / BAIT TYPE:
_____

COLOR: _____ SIZE: _____ MODEL: _____

ROD: _____ REEL:_____ LINE: _____

NOTES: _____

_____

SPECIES:_____ LENGTH: _____ WEIGHT: _____

TIME CAUGHT:_____ LOCATION:_____

STUCTURE/ VEGETATION: _____ DEPTH: _____
LURE / BAIT TYPE:
_____

COLOR: _____ SIZE: _____ MODEL: _____

ROD: _____ REEL:_____ LINE: _____

NOTES: _____

_____

SPECIES:_____ LENGTH: _____ WEIGHT: _____

TIME CAUGHT:_____ LOCATION:_____

STUCTURE/ VEGETATION: _____ DEPTH: _____
LURE / BAIT TYPE:
_____

COLOR: _____ SIZE: _____ MODEL: _____

ROD: _____ REEL:_____ LINE: _____

NOTES: _____

_____

SPECIES:_____ LENGTH: _____ WEIGHT: _____

TIME CAUGHT:_____ LOCATION:_____

STUCTURE/ VEGETATION: _____ DEPTH: _____
LURE / BAIT TYPE: _____

COLOR: _____ SIZE: _____ MODEL: _____

ROD: _____ REEL:_____ LINE: _____

NOTES: _____

_____

SPECIES:_____ LENGTH: _____ WEIGHT: _____

TIME CAUGHT:_____ LOCATION:_____

STUCTURE/ VEGETATION: _____ DEPTH: _____
LURE / BAIT TYPE: _____

COLOR: _____ SIZE: _____ MODEL: _____

ROD: _____ REEL:_____ LINE: _____

NOTES: _____

_____

SPECIES:_____ LENGTH: _____ WEIGHT: _____

TIME CAUGHT:_____ LOCATION:_____

STUCTURE/ VEGETATION: _____ DEPTH: _____
LURE / BAIT TYPE: _____

COLOR: _____ SIZE: _____ MODEL: _____

ROD: _____ REEL:_____ LINE: _____

NOTES: _____

_____

FISHING JOURNAL AND LOG BOOK

SPECIES BEING PURSUED _____

DATE: _____ TIME: _____ TO: _____

WHO I FISHED WITH: _____

WATER LOCATION DETAILS

BODY OF WATER: _____ LAUNCH RAMP: _____

WATER TEMP AT LAUNCH: _____ UPON RETURN : _____

WATER CLARITY:
☐ CLEAR ☐ STAINED ☐ MURKY ☐ MUDDY ☐ OTHER: _____

WATER LEVEL:
☐ NORMAL ☐ LOW ☐ HIGH ☐ DROPPING ☐ RISING

OTHER FACTORS:
☐ INSECT HATCHES ☐ BAIT FISH ☐ OTHER _____

WEATHER DETAILS

CURRENT AIR TEMP: _____ HIGH/LOW: _____ / _____

WIND SPEED: _____ DIRECTION: _____

MOON PHASE: _____ BAROMETER: _____

SUNRISE: _____ SUNSET: _____

CONDITIONS NOTED:
☐ SUNNY ☐ PARTLY CLOUDY ☐ CLOUDY ☐ STORM CLOUDS
☐ RAINING ☐ FOG ☐ DRIZZLE ☐ SLEET ☐ SNOW
☐ OTHER: _____

NOTES: _____
_____
_____

SPECIES:_____ LENGTH: _____ WEIGHT: _____

TIME CAUGHT:_____ LOCATION:_____

STUCTURE / VEGETATION: _____ DEPTH: _____
LURE / BAIT TYPE: _____

COLOR: _____ SIZE: _____ MODEL: _____

ROD: _____ REEL:_____ LINE: _____

NOTES: _____
_____

═══

SPECIES:_____ LENGTH: _____ WEIGHT: _____

TIME CAUGHT:_____ LOCATION:_____

STUCTURE / VEGETATION: _____ DEPTH: _____
LURE / BAIT TYPE: _____

COLOR: _____ SIZE: _____ MODEL: _____

ROD: _____ REEL:_____ LINE: _____

NOTES: _____
_____

═══

SPECIES:_____ LENGTH: _____ WEIGHT: _____

TIME CAUGHT:_____ LOCATION:_____

STUCTURE / VEGETATION: _____ DEPTH: _____
LURE / BAIT TYPE: _____

COLOR: _____ SIZE: _____ MODEL: _____

ROD: _____ REEL:_____ LINE: _____

NOTES: _____
_____

SPECIES:_____ LENGTH: _____ WEIGHT: _____

TIME CAUGHT:_____ LOCATION:_____

STUCTURE/ VEGETATION: _____ DEPTH: _____
LURE / BAIT TYPE: _____

COLOR: _____ SIZE: _____ MODEL: _____

ROD: _____ REEL:_____ LINE: _____

NOTES: _____
_____

SPECIES:_____ LENGTH: _____ WEIGHT: _____

TIME CAUGHT:_____ LOCATION:_____

STUCTURE/ VEGETATION: _____ DEPTH: _____
LURE / BAIT TYPE: _____

COLOR: _____ SIZE: _____ MODEL: _____

ROD: _____ REEL:_____ LINE: _____

NOTES: _____
_____

SPECIES:_____ LENGTH: _____ WEIGHT: _____

TIME CAUGHT:_____ LOCATION:_____

STUCTURE/ VEGETATION: _____ DEPTH: _____
LURE / BAIT TYPE: _____

COLOR: _____ SIZE: _____ MODEL: _____

ROD: _____ REEL:_____ LINE: _____

NOTES: _____
_____

SPECIES:_____ LENGTH: _____ WEIGHT: _____

TIME CAUGHT:_____ LOCATION:_____

STUCTURE/ VEGETATION: _____ DEPTH: _____
LURE / BAIT TYPE: _____

COLOR: _____ SIZE: _____ MODEL: _____

ROD: _____ REEL:_____ LINE: _____

NOTES: _____

_____

SPECIES:_____ LENGTH: _____ WEIGHT: _____

TIME CAUGHT:_____ LOCATION:_____

STUCTURE/ VEGETATION: _____ DEPTH: _____
LURE / BAIT TYPE: _____

COLOR: _____ SIZE: _____ MODEL: _____

ROD: _____ REEL:_____ LINE: _____

NOTES: _____

_____

SPECIES:_____ LENGTH: _____ WEIGHT: _____

TIME CAUGHT:_____ LOCATION:_____

STUCTURE/ VEGETATION: _____ DEPTH: _____
LURE / BAIT TYPE: _____

COLOR: _____ SIZE: _____ MODEL: _____

ROD: _____ REEL:_____ LINE: _____

NOTES: _____

_____

SPECIES:_____ LENGTH: _____ WEIGHT: _____

TIME CAUGHT:_____ LOCATION:_____

STUCTURE/ VEGETATION: _____ DEPTH: _____
LURE / BAIT TYPE: _____

COLOR: _____ SIZE: _____ MODEL: _____

ROD: _____ REEL:_____ LINE: _____

NOTES: _____

_____

SPECIES:_____ LENGTH: _____ WEIGHT: _____

TIME CAUGHT:_____ LOCATION:_____

STUCTURE/ VEGETATION: _____ DEPTH: _____
LURE / BAIT TYPE: _____

COLOR: _____ SIZE: _____ MODEL: _____

ROD: _____ REEL:_____ LINE: _____

NOTES: _____

_____

SPECIES:_____ LENGTH: _____ WEIGHT: _____

TIME CAUGHT:_____ LOCATION:_____

STUCTURE/ VEGETATION: _____ DEPTH: _____
LURE / BAIT TYPE: _____

COLOR: _____ SIZE: _____ MODEL: _____

ROD: _____ REEL:_____ LINE: _____

NOTES: _____

_____

FISHING JOURNAL AND LOG BOOK

SPECIES BEING PURSUED _____

DATE: _____ TIME: _____ TO: _____

WHO I FISHED WITH: _____

WATER LOCATION DETAILS
BODY OF WATER: _____ LAUNCH RAMP: _____

WATER TEMP AT LAUNCH: _____ UPON RETURN : _____

WATER CLARITY:
☐ CLEAR ☐ STAINED ☐ MURKY ☐ MUDDY ☐ OTHER: _____

WATER LEVEL:
☐ NORMAL ☐ LOW ☐ HIGH ☐ DROPPING ☐ RISING

OTHER FACTORS:
☐ INSECT HATCHES ☐ BAIT FISH ☐ OTHER _____

WEATHER DETAILS
CURRENT AIR TEMP: _____ HIGH/LOW: _____/_____

WIND SPEED: _____ DIRECTION: _____

MOON PHASE: _____ BAROMETER: _____

SUNRISE: _____ SUNSET: _____

CONDITIONS NOTED:
☐ SUNNY ☐ PARTLY CLOUDY ☐ CLOUDY ☐ STORM CLOUDS
☐ RAINING ☐ FOG ☐ DRIZZLE ☐ SLEET ☐ SNOW
☐ OTHER: _____

NOTES: _____

_____

_____

SPECIES:_____ LENGTH:_____ WEIGHT:_____

TIME CAUGHT:_____ LOCATION:_____

STUCTURE/ VEGETATION: _____ DEPTH:_____
LURE / BAIT TYPE: _____

COLOR: _____ SIZE: _____ MODEL: _____

ROD: _____ REEL:_____ LINE: _____

NOTES: _____
_____

SPECIES:_____ LENGTH:_____ WEIGHT:_____

TIME CAUGHT:_____ LOCATION:_____

STUCTURE/ VEGETATION: _____ DEPTH:_____
LURE / BAIT TYPE: _____

COLOR: _____ SIZE: _____ MODEL: _____

ROD: _____ REEL:_____ LINE: _____

NOTES: _____
_____

SPECIES:_____ LENGTH:_____ WEIGHT:_____

TIME CAUGHT:_____ LOCATION:_____

STUCTURE/ VEGETATION: _____ DEPTH:_____
LURE / BAIT TYPE: _____

COLOR: _____ SIZE: _____ MODEL: _____

ROD: _____ REEL:_____ LINE: _____

NOTES: _____
_____

SPECIES:_____ LENGTH:_____ WEIGHT:_____

TIME CAUGHT:_____ LOCATION:_____

STUCTURE/ VEGETATION: _____ DEPTH:_____
LURE / BAIT TYPE: _____

COLOR: _____ SIZE: _____ MODEL: _____

ROD: _____ REEL:_____ LINE: _____

NOTES: _____

_____

SPECIES:_____ LENGTH:_____ WEIGHT:_____

TIME CAUGHT:_____ LOCATION:_____

STUCTURE/ VEGETATION: _____ DEPTH:_____
LURE / BAIT TYPE: _____

COLOR: _____ SIZE: _____ MODEL: _____

ROD: _____ REEL:_____ LINE: _____

NOTES: _____

_____

SPECIES:_____ LENGTH:_____ WEIGHT:_____

TIME CAUGHT:_____ LOCATION:_____

STUCTURE/ VEGETATION: _____ DEPTH:_____
LURE / BAIT TYPE: _____

COLOR: _____ SIZE: _____ MODEL: _____

ROD: _____ REEL:_____ LINE: _____

NOTES: _____

_____

SPECIES:_____ LENGTH:_____ WEIGHT:_____

TIME CAUGHT:_____ LOCATION:_____

STUCTURE/ VEGETATION: _____ DEPTH:_____
LURE / BAIT TYPE: _____

COLOR:_____ SIZE:_____ MODEL:_____

ROD:_____ REEL:_____ LINE:_____

NOTES: _____
_____

SPECIES:_____ LENGTH:_____ WEIGHT:_____

TIME CAUGHT:_____ LOCATION:_____

STUCTURE/ VEGETATION: _____ DEPTH:_____
LURE / BAIT TYPE: _____

COLOR:_____ SIZE:_____ MODEL:_____

ROD:_____ REEL:_____ LINE:_____

NOTES: _____
_____

SPECIES:_____ LENGTH:_____ WEIGHT:_____

TIME CAUGHT:_____ LOCATION:_____

STUCTURE/ VEGETATION: _____ DEPTH:_____
LURE / BAIT TYPE: _____

COLOR:_____ SIZE:_____ MODEL:_____

ROD:_____ REEL:_____ LINE:_____

NOTES: _____
_____

SPECIES:_____ LENGTH:_____ WEIGHT:_____

TIME CAUGHT:_____ LOCATION:_____

STUCTURE/ VEGETATION: _____ DEPTH:_____
LURE / BAIT TYPE: _____

COLOR: _____ SIZE: _____ MODEL: _____

ROD: _____ REEL:_____ LINE: _____

NOTES: _____
_____

═══

SPECIES:_____ LENGTH:_____ WEIGHT:_____

TIME CAUGHT:_____ LOCATION:_____

STUCTURE/ VEGETATION: _____ DEPTH:_____
LURE / BAIT TYPE: _____

COLOR: _____ SIZE: _____ MODEL: _____

ROD: _____ REEL:_____ LINE: _____

NOTES: _____
_____

═══

SPECIES:_____ LENGTH:_____ WEIGHT:_____

TIME CAUGHT:_____ LOCATION:_____

STUCTURE/ VEGETATION: _____ DEPTH:_____
LURE / BAIT TYPE: _____

COLOR: _____ SIZE: _____ MODEL: _____

ROD: _____ REEL:_____ LINE: _____

NOTES: _____
_____

FISHING JOURNAL AND LOG BOOK

SPECIES BEING PURSUED _____

DATE: _____   TIME: _____   TO: _____

WHO I FISHED WITH: _____

WATER LOCATION DETAILS

BODY OF WATER: _____   LAUNCH RAMP: _____

WATER TEMP AT LAUNCH: _____   UPON RETURN : _____

WATER CLARITY:
☐ CLEAR   ☐ STAINED   ☐ MURKY   ☐ MUDDY   ☐ OTHER: _____

WATER LEVEL:
☐ NORMAL   ☐ LOW   ☐ HIGH   ☐ DROPPING   ☐ RISING

OTHER FACTORS:
☐ INSECT HATCHES   ☐ BAIT FISH   ☐ OTHER_____

WEATHER DETAILS

CURRENT AIR TEMP: _____   HIGH/LOW: _____ / _____
WIND SPEED: _____   DIRECTION: _____
MOON PHASE: _____   BAROMETER: _____
SUNRISE: _____   SUNSET: _____

CONDITIONS NOTED:
☐ SUNNY   ☐ PARTLY CLOUDY   ☐ CLOUDY   ☐ STORM CLOUDS
☐ RAINING   ☐ FOG   ☐ DRIZZLE   ☐ SLEET   ☐ SNOW
☐ OTHER: _____

NOTES: _____
_____
_____

SPECIES:_____ LENGTH:_____ WEIGHT:_____

TIME CAUGHT:_____ LOCATION:_____

STUCTURE/ VEGETATION: _____ DEPTH:_____
LURE / BAIT TYPE: _____

COLOR: _____ SIZE: _____ MODEL: _____

ROD: _____ REEL:_____ LINE: _____

NOTES: _____
_____

SPECIES:_____ LENGTH:_____ WEIGHT:_____

TIME CAUGHT:_____ LOCATION:_____

STUCTURE/ VEGETATION: _____ DEPTH:_____
LURE / BAIT TYPE: _____

COLOR: _____ SIZE: _____ MODEL: _____

ROD: _____ REEL:_____ LINE: _____

NOTES: _____
_____

SPECIES:_____ LENGTH:_____ WEIGHT:_____

TIME CAUGHT:_____ LOCATION:_____

STUCTURE/ VEGETATION: _____ DEPTH:_____
LURE / BAIT TYPE: _____

COLOR: _____ SIZE: _____ MODEL: _____

ROD: _____ REEL:_____ LINE: _____

NOTES: _____
_____

SPECIES:_____ LENGTH: _____ WEIGHT: _____

TIME CAUGHT:_____ LOCATION:_____

STUCTURE/ VEGETATION: _____ DEPTH: _____
LURE / BAIT TYPE: _____

COLOR: _____ SIZE: _____ MODEL: _____

ROD: _____ REEL:_____ LINE: _____

NOTES: _____
_____

═══════════════════════════════

SPECIES:_____ LENGTH: _____ WEIGHT: _____

TIME CAUGHT:_____ LOCATION:_____

STUCTURE/ VEGETATION: _____ DEPTH: _____
LURE / BAIT TYPE: _____

COLOR: _____ SIZE: _____ MODEL: _____

ROD: _____ REEL:_____ LINE: _____

NOTES: _____
_____

═══════════════════════════════

SPECIES:_____ LENGTH: _____ WEIGHT: _____

TIME CAUGHT:_____ LOCATION:_____

STUCTURE/ VEGETATION: _____ DEPTH: _____
LURE / BAIT TYPE: _____

COLOR: _____ SIZE: _____ MODEL: _____

ROD: _____ REEL:_____ LINE: _____

NOTES: _____
_____

SPECIES:_____ LENGTH:_____ WEIGHT:_____

TIME CAUGHT:_____ LOCATION:_____

STUCTURE/ VEGETATION: _____ DEPTH:_____
LURE / BAIT TYPE: _____

COLOR: _____ SIZE: _____ MODEL: _____

ROD: _____ REEL:_____ LINE: _____

NOTES: _____
_____

SPECIES:_____ LENGTH:_____ WEIGHT:_____

TIME CAUGHT:_____ LOCATION:_____

STUCTURE/ VEGETATION: _____ DEPTH:_____
LURE / BAIT TYPE: _____

COLOR: _____ SIZE: _____ MODEL: _____

ROD: _____ REEL:_____ LINE: _____

NOTES: _____
_____

SPECIES:_____ LENGTH:_____ WEIGHT:_____

TIME CAUGHT:_____ LOCATION:_____

STUCTURE/ VEGETATION: _____ DEPTH:_____
LURE / BAIT TYPE: _____

COLOR: _____ SIZE: _____ MODEL: _____

ROD: _____ REEL:_____ LINE: _____

NOTES: _____
_____

SPECIES:_____ LENGTH:_____ WEIGHT: _____

TIME CAUGHT:_____ LOCATION:_____

STUCTURE/ VEGETATION: _____ DEPTH: _____
LURE / BAIT TYPE: _____

COLOR: _____ SIZE: _____ MODEL: _____

ROD: _____ REEL:_____ LINE: _____

NOTES: _____
_____

═══════════════════════════════════════

SPECIES:_____ LENGTH:_____ WEIGHT: _____

TIME CAUGHT:_____ LOCATION:_____

STUCTURE/ VEGETATION: _____ DEPTH: _____
LURE / BAIT TYPE: _____

COLOR: _____ SIZE: _____ MODEL: _____

ROD: _____ REEL:_____ LINE: _____

NOTES: _____
_____

═══════════════════════════════════════

SPECIES:_____ LENGTH:_____ WEIGHT: _____

TIME CAUGHT:_____ LOCATION:_____

STUCTURE/ VEGETATION: _____ DEPTH: _____
LURE / BAIT TYPE: _____

COLOR: _____ SIZE: _____ MODEL: _____

ROD: _____ REEL:_____ LINE: _____

NOTES: _____
_____

FISHING JOURNAL AND LOG BOOK

SPECIES BEING PURSUED _____

DATE: _____   TIME: _____   TO: _____

WHO I FISHED WITH: _____

WATER LOCATION DETAILS
BODY OF WATER: _____   LAUNCH RAMP: _____

WATER TEMP AT LAUNCH: _____   UPON RETURN : _____

WATER CLARITY:
☐ CLEAR ☐ STAINED ☐ MURKY ☐ MUDDY ☐ OTHER: _____

WATER LEVEL:
☐ NORMAL ☐ LOW ☐ HIGH ☐ DROPPING ☐ RISING

OTHER FACTORS:
☐ INSECT HATCHES ☐ BAIT FISH ☐ OTHER_____

WEATHER DETAILS
CURRENT AIR TEMP: _____   HIGH/LOW: _____ / _____
WIND SPEED: _____   DIRECTION: _____
MOON PHASE: _____   BAROMETER: _____
SUNRISE: _____   SUNSET: _____

CONDITIONS NOTED:
☐ SUNNY ☐ PARTLY CLOUDY ☐ CLOUDY ☐ STORM CLOUDS
☐ RAINING ☐ FOG ☐ DRIZZLE ☐ SLEET ☐ SNOW
☐ OTHER: _____

NOTES: _____
_____
_____

SPECIES:_____ LENGTH:_____ WEIGHT:_____

TIME CAUGHT:_____ LOCATION:_____

STUCTURE/ VEGETATION: _____ DEPTH:_____
LURE / BAIT TYPE: _____

COLOR: _____ SIZE: _____ MODEL: _____

ROD: _____ REEL:_____ LINE: _____

NOTES: _____

_____

═══

SPECIES:_____ LENGTH:_____ WEIGHT:_____

TIME CAUGHT:_____ LOCATION:_____

STUCTURE/ VEGETATION: _____ DEPTH:_____
LURE / BAIT TYPE: _____

COLOR: _____ SIZE: _____ MODEL: _____

ROD: _____ REEL:_____ LINE: _____

NOTES: _____

_____

═══

SPECIES:_____ LENGTH:_____ WEIGHT:_____

TIME CAUGHT:_____ LOCATION:_____

STUCTURE/ VEGETATION: _____ DEPTH:_____
LURE / BAIT TYPE: _____

COLOR: _____ SIZE: _____ MODEL: _____

ROD: _____ REEL:_____ LINE: _____

NOTES: _____

_____

SPECIES:_____ LENGTH:_____ WEIGHT:_____

TIME CAUGHT:_____ LOCATION:_____

STUCTURE/ VEGETATION: _____ DEPTH:_____
LURE / BAIT TYPE: _____

COLOR:_____ SIZE:_____ MODEL:_____

ROD:_____ REEL:_____ LINE:_____

NOTES: _____
_____

SPECIES:_____ LENGTH:_____ WEIGHT:_____

TIME CAUGHT:_____ LOCATION:_____

STUCTURE/ VEGETATION: _____ DEPTH:_____
LURE / BAIT TYPE: _____

COLOR:_____ SIZE:_____ MODEL:_____

ROD:_____ REEL:_____ LINE:_____

NOTES: _____
_____

SPECIES:_____ LENGTH:_____ WEIGHT:_____

TIME CAUGHT:_____ LOCATION:_____

STUCTURE/ VEGETATION: _____ DEPTH:_____
LURE / BAIT TYPE: _____

COLOR:_____ SIZE:_____ MODEL:_____

ROD:_____ REEL:_____ LINE:_____

NOTES: _____
_____

SPECIES:_____ LENGTH:_____ WEIGHT:_____

TIME CAUGHT:_____ LOCATION:_____

STUCTURE/ VEGETATION: _____ DEPTH:_____
LURE / BAIT TYPE: _____

COLOR: _____ SIZE: _____ MODEL: _____

ROD: _____ REEL:_____ LINE: _____

NOTES: _____
_____

═══════════════════════════════════════

SPECIES:_____ LENGTH:_____ WEIGHT:_____

TIME CAUGHT:_____ LOCATION:_____

STUCTURE/ VEGETATION: _____ DEPTH:_____
LURE / BAIT TYPE: _____

COLOR: _____ SIZE: _____ MODEL: _____

ROD: _____ REEL:_____ LINE: _____

NOTES: _____
_____

═══════════════════════════════════════

SPECIES:_____ LENGTH:_____ WEIGHT:_____

TIME CAUGHT:_____ LOCATION:_____

STUCTURE/ VEGETATION: _____ DEPTH:_____
LURE / BAIT TYPE: _____

COLOR: _____ SIZE: _____ MODEL: _____

ROD: _____ REEL:_____ LINE: _____

NOTES: _____
_____

SPECIES:_____ LENGTH:_____ WEIGHT:_____

TIME CAUGHT:_____ LOCATION:_____

STUCTURE/ VEGETATION: _____ DEPTH:_____
LURE / BAIT TYPE: _____

COLOR:_____ SIZE:_____ MODEL:_____

ROD:_____ REEL:_____ LINE:_____

NOTES: _____
_____

═══

SPECIES:_____ LENGTH:_____ WEIGHT:_____

TIME CAUGHT:_____ LOCATION:_____

STUCTURE/ VEGETATION: _____ DEPTH:_____
LURE / BAIT TYPE: _____

COLOR:_____ SIZE:_____ MODEL:_____

ROD:_____ REEL:_____ LINE:_____

NOTES: _____
_____

═══

SPECIES:_____ LENGTH:_____ WEIGHT:_____

TIME CAUGHT:_____ LOCATION:_____

STUCTURE/ VEGETATION: _____ DEPTH:_____
LURE / BAIT TYPE: _____

COLOR:_____ SIZE:_____ MODEL:_____

ROD:_____ REEL:_____ LINE:_____

NOTES: _____
_____

FISHING JOURNAL AND LOG BOOK

SPECIES BEING PURSUED _____

DATE: _____ TIME: _____ TO: _____

WHO I FISHED WITH: _____

WATER LOCATION DETAILS

BODY OF WATER: _____ LAUNCH RAMP: _____

WATER TEMP AT LAUNCH: _____ UPON RETURN : _____

WATER CLARITY:
☐ CLEAR ☐ STAINED ☐ MURKY ☐ MUDDY ☐ OTHER: _____

WATER LEVEL:
☐ NORMAL ☐ LOW ☐ HIGH ☐ DROPPING ☐ RISING

OTHER FACTORS:
☐ INSECT HATCHES ☐ BAIT FISH ☐ OTHER_____

WEATHER DETAILS

CURRENT AIR TEMP: _____ HIGH/LOW: _____/_____

WIND SPEED: _____ DIRECTION: _____

MOON PHASE: _____ BAROMETER: _____

SUNRISE: _____ SUNSET: _____

CONDITIONS NOTED:
☐ SUNNY ☐ PARTLY CLOUDY ☐ CLOUDY ☐ STORM CLOUDS
☐ RAINING ☐ FOG ☐ DRIZZLE ☐ SLEET ☐ SNOW
☐ OTHER: _____

NOTES: _____

_____

_____

SPECIES:_____ LENGTH:_____ WEIGHT:_____

TIME CAUGHT:_____ LOCATION:_____

STUCTURE/ VEGETATION: _____ DEPTH:_____
LURE / BAIT TYPE:
_____

COLOR: _____ SIZE: _____ MODEL: _____

ROD: _____ REEL:_____ LINE: _____

NOTES: _____

_____

SPECIES:_____ LENGTH:_____ WEIGHT:_____

TIME CAUGHT:_____ LOCATION:_____

STUCTURE/ VEGETATION: _____ DEPTH:_____
LURE / BAIT TYPE:
_____

COLOR: _____ SIZE: _____ MODEL: _____

ROD: _____ REEL:_____ LINE: _____

NOTES: _____

_____

SPECIES:_____ LENGTH:_____ WEIGHT:_____

TIME CAUGHT:_____ LOCATION:_____

STUCTURE/ VEGETATION: _____ DEPTH:_____
LURE / BAIT TYPE:
_____

COLOR: _____ SIZE: _____ MODEL: _____

ROD: _____ REEL:_____ LINE: _____

NOTES: _____

_____

SPECIES:_____ LENGTH: _____ WEIGHT: _____

TIME CAUGHT:_____ LOCATION:_____

STUCTURE/ VEGETATION: _____ DEPTH: _____

LURE / BAIT TYPE: _____

COLOR: _____ SIZE: _____ MODEL: _____

ROD: _____ REEL:_____ LINE: _____

NOTES: _____

_____

SPECIES:_____ LENGTH: _____ WEIGHT: _____

TIME CAUGHT:_____ LOCATION:_____

STUCTURE/ VEGETATION: _____ DEPTH: _____

LURE / BAIT TYPE: _____

COLOR: _____ SIZE: _____ MODEL: _____

ROD: _____ REEL:_____ LINE: _____

NOTES: _____

_____

SPECIES:_____ LENGTH: _____ WEIGHT: _____

TIME CAUGHT:_____ LOCATION:_____

STUCTURE/ VEGETATION: _____ DEPTH: _____

LURE / BAIT TYPE: _____

COLOR: _____ SIZE: _____ MODEL: _____

ROD: _____ REEL:_____ LINE: _____

NOTES: _____

_____

SPECIES:_____ LENGTH:_____ WEIGHT:_____

TIME CAUGHT:_____ LOCATION:_____

STUCTURE/ VEGETATION: _____ DEPTH:_____
LURE / BAIT TYPE:_____

COLOR: _____ SIZE: _____ MODEL: _____

ROD: _____ REEL:_____ LINE: _____

NOTES: _____

_____

SPECIES:_____ LENGTH:_____ WEIGHT:_____

TIME CAUGHT:_____ LOCATION:_____

STUCTURE/ VEGETATION: _____ DEPTH:_____
LURE / BAIT TYPE:_____

COLOR: _____ SIZE: _____ MODEL: _____

ROD: _____ REEL:_____ LINE: _____

NOTES: _____

_____

SPECIES:_____ LENGTH:_____ WEIGHT:_____

TIME CAUGHT:_____ LOCATION:_____

STUCTURE/ VEGETATION: _____ DEPTH:_____
LURE / BAIT TYPE:_____

COLOR: _____ SIZE: _____ MODEL: _____

ROD: _____ REEL:_____ LINE: _____

NOTES: _____

_____

SPECIES:_____ LENGTH:_____ WEIGHT:_____

TIME CAUGHT:_____ LOCATION:_____

STUCTURE/ VEGETATION:_____ DEPTH:_____
LURE / BAIT TYPE:_____

COLOR:_____ SIZE:_____ MODEL:_____

ROD:_____ REEL:_____ LINE:_____

NOTES:_____
_____

SPECIES:_____ LENGTH:_____ WEIGHT:_____

TIME CAUGHT:_____ LOCATION:_____

STUCTURE/ VEGETATION:_____ DEPTH:_____
LURE / BAIT TYPE:_____

COLOR:_____ SIZE:_____ MODEL:_____

ROD:_____ REEL:_____ LINE:_____

NOTES:_____
_____

SPECIES:_____ LENGTH:_____ WEIGHT:_____

TIME CAUGHT:_____ LOCATION:_____

STUCTURE/ VEGETATION:_____ DEPTH:_____
LURE / BAIT TYPE:_____

COLOR:_____ SIZE:_____ MODEL:_____

ROD:_____ REEL:_____ LINE:_____

NOTES:_____
_____

FISHING JOURNAL AND LOG BOOK

SPECIES BEING PURSUED _____

DATE: _____   TIME: _____   TO: _____

WHO I FISHED WITH: _____

WATER LOCATION DETAILS
BODY OF WATER: _____ LAUNCH RAMP: _____

WATER TEMP AT LAUNCH: _____ UPON RETURN : _____

WATER CLARITY:
☐ CLEAR   ☐ STAINED   ☐ MURKY   ☐ MUDDY   ☐ OTHER: _____

WATER LEVEL:
☐ NORMAL   ☐ LOW   ☐ HIGH   ☐ DROPPING   ☐ RISING

OTHER FACTORS:
☐ INSECT HATCHES   ☐ BAIT FISH   ☐ OTHER_____

WEATHER DETAILS
CURRENT AIR TEMP: _____ HIGH/LOW: _____ / _____

WIND SPEED: _____ DIRECTION: _____

MOON PHASE: _____ BAROMETER: _____

SUNRISE: _____ SUNSET: _____

CONDITIONS NOTED:
☐ SUNNY   ☐ PARTLY CLOUDY   ☐ CLOUDY   ☐ STORM CLOUDS
☐ RAINING   ☐ FOG   ☐ DRIZZLE   ☐ SLEET   ☐ SNOW
☐ OTHER: _____

NOTES: _____

_____

_____

SPECIES:_____ LENGTH:_____ WEIGHT:_____

TIME CAUGHT:_____ LOCATION:_____

STUCTURE/ VEGETATION: _____ DEPTH:_____
LURE / BAIT TYPE: _____

COLOR: _____ SIZE: _____ MODEL: _____

ROD: _____ REEL:_____ LINE: _____

NOTES: _____
_____

SPECIES:_____ LENGTH:_____ WEIGHT:_____

TIME CAUGHT:_____ LOCATION:_____

STUCTURE/ VEGETATION: _____ DEPTH:_____
LURE / BAIT TYPE: _____

COLOR: _____ SIZE: _____ MODEL: _____

ROD: _____ REEL:_____ LINE: _____

NOTES: _____
_____

SPECIES:_____ LENGTH:_____ WEIGHT:_____

TIME CAUGHT:_____ LOCATION:_____

STUCTURE/ VEGETATION: _____ DEPTH:_____
LURE / BAIT TYPE: _____

COLOR: _____ SIZE: _____ MODEL: _____

ROD: _____ REEL:_____ LINE: _____

NOTES: _____
_____

SPECIES:_____ LENGTH: _____ WEIGHT: _____

TIME CAUGHT:_____ LOCATION:_____

STUCTURE/ VEGETATION: _____ DEPTH: _____
LURE / BAIT TYPE: _____

COLOR: _____ SIZE: _____ MODEL: _____

ROD: _____ REEL:_____ LINE: _____

NOTES: _____
_____

SPECIES:_____ LENGTH: _____ WEIGHT: _____

TIME CAUGHT:_____ LOCATION:_____

STUCTURE/ VEGETATION: _____ DEPTH: _____
LURE / BAIT TYPE: _____

COLOR: _____ SIZE: _____ MODEL: _____

ROD: _____ REEL:_____ LINE: _____

NOTES: _____
_____

SPECIES:_____ LENGTH: _____ WEIGHT: _____

TIME CAUGHT:_____ LOCATION:_____

STUCTURE/ VEGETATION: _____ DEPTH: _____
LURE / BAIT TYPE: _____

COLOR: _____ SIZE: _____ MODEL: _____

ROD: _____ REEL:_____ LINE: _____

NOTES: _____
_____

SPECIES:_____ LENGTH:_____ WEIGHT:_____

TIME CAUGHT:_____ LOCATION:_____

STUCTURE/ VEGETATION:_____ DEPTH:_____
LURE / BAIT TYPE:_____

COLOR:_____ SIZE:_____ MODEL:_____

ROD:_____ REEL:_____ LINE:_____

NOTES:_____
_____

SPECIES:_____ LENGTH:_____ WEIGHT:_____

TIME CAUGHT:_____ LOCATION:_____

STUCTURE/ VEGETATION:_____ DEPTH:_____
LURE / BAIT TYPE:_____

COLOR:_____ SIZE:_____ MODEL:_____

ROD:_____ REEL:_____ LINE:_____

NOTES:_____
_____

SPECIES:_____ LENGTH:_____ WEIGHT:_____

TIME CAUGHT:_____ LOCATION:_____

STUCTURE/ VEGETATION:_____ DEPTH:_____
LURE / BAIT TYPE:_____

COLOR:_____ SIZE:_____ MODEL:_____

ROD:_____ REEL:_____ LINE:_____

NOTES:_____
_____

SPECIES:_____ LENGTH:_____ WEIGHT:_____

TIME CAUGHT:_____ LOCATION:_____

STUCTURE/ VEGETATION: _____ DEPTH:_____
LURE / BAIT TYPE: _____

COLOR: _____ SIZE: _____ MODEL: _____

ROD: _____ REEL:_____ LINE: _____

NOTES: _____
_____

SPECIES:_____ LENGTH:_____ WEIGHT:_____

TIME CAUGHT:_____ LOCATION:_____

STUCTURE/ VEGETATION: _____ DEPTH:_____
LURE / BAIT TYPE: _____

COLOR: _____ SIZE: _____ MODEL: _____

ROD: _____ REEL:_____ LINE: _____

NOTES: _____
_____

SPECIES:_____ LENGTH:_____ WEIGHT:_____

TIME CAUGHT:_____ LOCATION:_____

STUCTURE/ VEGETATION: _____ DEPTH:_____
LURE / BAIT TYPE: _____

COLOR: _____ SIZE: _____ MODEL: _____

ROD: _____ REEL:_____ LINE: _____

NOTES: _____
_____

FISHING JOURNAL AND LOG BOOK

SPECIES BEING PURSUED _____

DATE: _____ TIME: _____ TO: _____

WHO I FISHED WITH: _____

WATER LOCATION DETAILS
BODY OF WATER: _____ LAUNCH RAMP: _____

WATER TEMP AT LAUNCH: _____ UPON RETURN : _____

WATER CLARITY:
☐ CLEAR ☐ STAINED ☐ MURKY ☐ MUDDY ☐ OTHER: _____

WATER LEVEL:
☐ NORMAL ☐ LOW ☐ HIGH ☐ DROPPING ☐ RISING

OTHER FACTORS:
☐ INSECT HATCHES ☐ BAIT FISH ☐ OTHER _____

WEATHER DETAILS
CURRENT AIR TEMP: _____ HIGH/LOW: _____ / _____

WIND SPEED: _____ DIRECTION: _____

MOON PHASE: _____ BAROMETER: _____

SUNRISE: _____ SUNSET: _____

CONDITIONS NOTED:
☐ SUNNY ☐ PARTLY CLOUDY ☐ CLOUDY ☐ STORM CLOUDS
☐ RAINING ☐ FOG ☐ DRIZZLE ☐ SLEET ☐ SNOW
☐ OTHER: _____

NOTES: _____

_____

_____

SPECIES:_____ LENGTH: _____ WEIGHT: _____

TIME CAUGHT:_____ LOCATION:_____

STUCTURE/ VEGETATION: _____ DEPTH: _____
LURE / BAIT TYPE: _____

COLOR: _____ SIZE: _____ MODEL: _____

ROD: _____ REEL:_____ LINE: _____

NOTES: _____

_____

SPECIES:_____ LENGTH: _____ WEIGHT: _____

TIME CAUGHT:_____ LOCATION:_____

STUCTURE/ VEGETATION: _____ DEPTH: _____
LURE / BAIT TYPE: _____

COLOR: _____ SIZE: _____ MODEL: _____

ROD: _____ REEL:_____ LINE: _____

NOTES: _____

_____

SPECIES:_____ LENGTH: _____ WEIGHT: _____

TIME CAUGHT:_____ LOCATION:_____

STUCTURE/ VEGETATION: _____ DEPTH: _____
LURE / BAIT TYPE: _____

COLOR: _____ SIZE: _____ MODEL: _____

ROD: _____ REEL:_____ LINE: _____

NOTES: _____

_____

SPECIES:_____ LENGTH:_____ WEIGHT: _____

TIME CAUGHT:_____ LOCATION:_____

STUCTURE/ VEGETATION: _____ DEPTH: _____
LURE / BAIT TYPE: _____

COLOR: _____ SIZE: _____ MODEL: _____

ROD: _____ REEL:_____ LINE: _____

NOTES: _____
_____

SPECIES:_____ LENGTH:_____ WEIGHT: _____

TIME CAUGHT:_____ LOCATION:_____

STUCTURE/ VEGETATION: _____ DEPTH: _____
LURE / BAIT TYPE: _____

COLOR: _____ SIZE: _____ MODEL: _____

ROD: _____ REEL:_____ LINE: _____

NOTES: _____
_____

SPECIES:_____ LENGTH:_____ WEIGHT: _____

TIME CAUGHT:_____ LOCATION:_____

STUCTURE/ VEGETATION: _____ DEPTH: _____
LURE / BAIT TYPE: _____

COLOR: _____ SIZE: _____ MODEL: _____

ROD: _____ REEL:_____ LINE: _____

NOTES: _____
_____

SPECIES:_____ LENGTH: _____ WEIGHT: _____

TIME CAUGHT:_____ LOCATION:_____

STUCTURE/ VEGETATION: _____ DEPTH: _____
LURE / BAIT TYPE: _____

COLOR: _____ SIZE: _____ MODEL: _____

ROD: _____ REEL:_____ LINE: _____

NOTES: _____

_____

SPECIES:_____ LENGTH: _____ WEIGHT: _____

TIME CAUGHT:_____ LOCATION:_____

STUCTURE/ VEGETATION: _____ DEPTH: _____
LURE / BAIT TYPE: _____

COLOR: _____ SIZE: _____ MODEL: _____

ROD: _____ REEL:_____ LINE: _____

NOTES: _____

_____

SPECIES:_____ LENGTH: _____ WEIGHT: _____

TIME CAUGHT:_____ LOCATION:_____

STUCTURE/ VEGETATION: _____ DEPTH: _____
LURE / BAIT TYPE: _____

COLOR: _____ SIZE: _____ MODEL: _____

ROD: _____ REEL:_____ LINE: _____

NOTES: _____

_____

SPECIES:_____ LENGTH:_____ WEIGHT:_____

TIME CAUGHT:_____ LOCATION:_____

STUCTURE/ VEGETATION: _____ DEPTH:_____
LURE / BAIT TYPE: _____

COLOR: _____ SIZE: _____ MODEL: _____

ROD: _____ REEL:_____ LINE:_____

NOTES: _____
_____

═══════════════════════════════════════

SPECIES:_____ LENGTH:_____ WEIGHT:_____

TIME CAUGHT:_____ LOCATION:_____

STUCTURE/ VEGETATION: _____ DEPTH:_____
LURE / BAIT TYPE: _____

COLOR: _____ SIZE: _____ MODEL: _____

ROD: _____ REEL:_____ LINE:_____

NOTES: _____
_____

═══════════════════════════════════════

SPECIES:_____ LENGTH:_____ WEIGHT:_____

TIME CAUGHT:_____ LOCATION:_____

STUCTURE/ VEGETATION: _____ DEPTH:_____
LURE / BAIT TYPE: _____

COLOR: _____ SIZE: _____ MODEL: _____

ROD: _____ REEL:_____ LINE:_____

NOTES: _____
_____

FISHING JOURNAL AND LOG BOOK

SPECIES BEING PURSUED _____

DATE: _____   TIME: _____   TO: _____

WHO I FISHED WITH: _____

WATER LOCATION DETAILS

BODY OF WATER: _____   LAUNCH RAMP: _____

WATER TEMP AT LAUNCH: _____   UPON RETURN : _____

WATER CLARITY:
☐ CLEAR   ☐ STAINED   ☐ MURKY   ☐ MUDDY   ☐ OTHER: _____

WATER LEVEL:
☐ NORMAL   ☐ LOW   ☐ HIGH   ☐ DROPPING   ☐ RISING

OTHER FACTORS:
☐ INSECT HATCHES   ☐ BAIT FISH   ☐ OTHER_____

WEATHER DETAILS

CURRENT AIR TEMP: _____   HIGH/LOW: _____/_____
WIND SPEED: _____   DIRECTION: _____
MOON PHASE: _____   BAROMETER: _____
SUNRISE: _____   SUNSET: _____

CONDITIONS NOTED:
☐ SUNNY   ☐ PARTLY CLOUDY   ☐ CLOUDY   ☐ STORM CLOUDS
☐ RAINING   ☐ FOG   ☐ DRIZZLE   ☐ SLEET   ☐ SNOW
☐ OTHER: _____

NOTES: _____

_____

_____

SPECIES:_____ LENGTH:_____ WEIGHT: _____

TIME CAUGHT:_____ LOCATION:_____

STUCTURE / VEGETATION: _____ DEPTH: _____
LURE / BAIT TYPE: _____

COLOR: _____ SIZE: _____ MODEL: _____

ROD: _____ REEL:_____ LINE: _____

NOTES: _____
_____

SPECIES:_____ LENGTH:_____ WEIGHT: _____

TIME CAUGHT:_____ LOCATION:_____

STUCTURE / VEGETATION: _____ DEPTH: _____
LURE / BAIT TYPE: _____

COLOR: _____ SIZE: _____ MODEL: _____

ROD: _____ REEL:_____ LINE: _____

NOTES: _____
_____

SPECIES:_____ LENGTH:_____ WEIGHT: _____

TIME CAUGHT:_____ LOCATION:_____

STUCTURE / VEGETATION: _____ DEPTH: _____
LURE / BAIT TYPE: _____

COLOR: _____ SIZE: _____ MODEL: _____

ROD: _____ REEL:_____ LINE: _____

NOTES: _____
_____

SPECIES:_____ LENGTH:_____ WEIGHT:_____

TIME CAUGHT:_____ LOCATION:_____

STUCTURE/ VEGETATION: _____ DEPTH:_____
LURE / BAIT TYPE: _____

COLOR: _____ SIZE: _____ MODEL: _____

ROD: _____ REEL:_____ LINE: _____

NOTES: _____
_____

SPECIES:_____ LENGTH:_____ WEIGHT:_____

TIME CAUGHT:_____ LOCATION:_____

STUCTURE/ VEGETATION: _____ DEPTH:_____
LURE / BAIT TYPE: _____

COLOR: _____ SIZE: _____ MODEL: _____

ROD: _____ REEL:_____ LINE: _____

NOTES: _____
_____

SPECIES:_____ LENGTH:_____ WEIGHT:_____

TIME CAUGHT:_____ LOCATION:_____

STUCTURE/ VEGETATION: _____ DEPTH:_____
LURE / BAIT TYPE: _____

COLOR: _____ SIZE: _____ MODEL: _____

ROD: _____ REEL:_____ LINE: _____

NOTES: _____

SPECIES:_____ LENGTH:_____ WEIGHT:_____

TIME CAUGHT:_____ LOCATION:_____

STUCTURE/ VEGETATION: _____ DEPTH:_____
LURE / BAIT TYPE: _____

COLOR: _____ SIZE: _____ MODEL: _____

ROD: _____ REEL:_____ LINE:_____

NOTES: _____
_____

SPECIES:_____ LENGTH:_____ WEIGHT:_____

TIME CAUGHT:_____ LOCATION:_____

STUCTURE/ VEGETATION: _____ DEPTH:_____
LURE / BAIT TYPE: _____

COLOR: _____ SIZE: _____ MODEL: _____

ROD: _____ REEL:_____ LINE:_____

NOTES: _____
_____

SPECIES:_____ LENGTH:_____ WEIGHT:_____

TIME CAUGHT:_____ LOCATION:_____

STUCTURE/ VEGETATION: _____ DEPTH:_____
LURE / BAIT TYPE: _____

COLOR: _____ SIZE: _____ MODEL: _____

ROD: _____ REEL:_____ LINE:_____

NOTES: _____
_____

SPECIES:_____ LENGTH:_____ WEIGHT:_____

TIME CAUGHT:_____ LOCATION:_____

STUCTURE/ VEGETATION: _____ DEPTH:_____
LURE / BAIT TYPE: _____

COLOR: _____ SIZE: _____ MODEL: _____

ROD: _____ REEL:_____ LINE:_____

NOTES: _____

_____

SPECIES:_____ LENGTH:_____ WEIGHT:_____

TIME CAUGHT:_____ LOCATION:_____

STUCTURE/ VEGETATION: _____ DEPTH:_____
LURE / BAIT TYPE: _____

COLOR: _____ SIZE: _____ MODEL: _____

ROD: _____ REEL:_____ LINE:_____

NOTES: _____

_____

SPECIES:_____ LENGTH:_____ WEIGHT:_____

TIME CAUGHT:_____ LOCATION:_____

STUCTURE/ VEGETATION: _____ DEPTH:_____
LURE / BAIT TYPE: _____

COLOR: _____ SIZE: _____ MODEL: _____

ROD: _____ REEL:_____ LINE:_____

NOTES: _____

_____

FISHING JOURNAL AND LOG BOOK

SPECIES BEING PURSUED _____

DATE: _____   TIME: _____   TO: _____

WHO I FISHED WITH: _____

WATER LOCATION DETAILS
BODY OF WATER: _____ LAUNCH RAMP: _____

WATER TEMP AT LAUNCH: _____ UPON RETURN : _____

WATER CLARITY:
☐ CLEAR ☐ STAINED ☐ MURKY ☐ MUDDY ☐ OTHER: _____

WATER LEVEL:
☐ NORMAL ☐ LOW ☐ HIGH ☐ DROPPING ☐ RISING

OTHER FACTORS:
☐ INSECT HATCHES ☐ BAIT FISH ☐ OTHER_____

WEATHER DETAILS
CURRENT AIR TEMP: _____ HIGH/LOW: _____ / _____

WIND SPEED: _____ DIRECTION: _____

MOON PHASE: _____ BAROMETER: _____

SUNRISE: _____ SUNSET: _____

CONDITIONS NOTED:
☐ SUNNY ☐ PARTLY CLOUDY ☐ CLOUDY ☐ STORM CLOUDS
☐ RAINING ☐ FOG ☐ DRIZZLE ☐ SLEET ☐ SNOW
☐ OTHER: _____

NOTES: _____

_____

_____

SPECIES:_____ LENGTH:_____ WEIGHT: _____

TIME CAUGHT:_____ LOCATION:_____

STUCTURE/ VEGETATION: _____ DEPTH: _____
LURE / BAIT TYPE: _____

COLOR: _____ SIZE: _____ MODEL: _____

ROD: _____ REEL:_____ LINE: _____

NOTES: _____

_____

SPECIES:_____ LENGTH:_____ WEIGHT: _____

TIME CAUGHT:_____ LOCATION:_____

STUCTURE/ VEGETATION: _____ DEPTH: _____
LURE / BAIT TYPE: _____

COLOR: _____ SIZE: _____ MODEL: _____

ROD: _____ REEL:_____ LINE: _____

NOTES: _____

_____

SPECIES:_____ LENGTH:_____ WEIGHT: _____

TIME CAUGHT:_____ LOCATION:_____

STUCTURE/ VEGETATION: _____ DEPTH: _____
LURE / BAIT TYPE: _____

COLOR: _____ SIZE: _____ MODEL: _____

ROD: _____ REEL:_____ LINE: _____

NOTES: _____

_____

SPECIES:_____ LENGTH: _____ WEIGHT: _____

TIME CAUGHT:_____ LOCATION:_____

STUCTURE/ VEGETATION: _____ DEPTH: _____
LURE / BAIT TYPE: _____

COLOR: _____ SIZE: _____ MODEL: _____

ROD: _____ REEL:_____ LINE: _____

NOTES: _____
_____

SPECIES:_____ LENGTH: _____ WEIGHT: _____

TIME CAUGHT:_____ LOCATION:_____

STUCTURE/ VEGETATION: _____ DEPTH: _____
LURE / BAIT TYPE: _____

COLOR: _____ SIZE: _____ MODEL: _____

ROD: _____ REEL:_____ LINE: _____

NOTES: _____
_____

SPECIES:_____ LENGTH: _____ WEIGHT: _____

TIME CAUGHT:_____ LOCATION:_____

STUCTURE/ VEGETATION: _____ DEPTH: _____
LURE / BAIT TYPE: _____

COLOR: _____ SIZE: _____ MODEL: _____

ROD: _____ REEL:_____ LINE: _____

NOTES: _____
_____

SPECIES:_____ LENGTH:_____ WEIGHT:_____

TIME CAUGHT:_____ LOCATION:_____

STUCTURE/ VEGETATION: _____ DEPTH:_____
LURE / BAIT TYPE: _____

COLOR: _____ SIZE: _____ MODEL: _____

ROD: _____ REEL:_____ LINE: _____

NOTES: _____

_____

═══

SPECIES:_____ LENGTH:_____ WEIGHT:_____

TIME CAUGHT:_____ LOCATION:_____

STUCTURE/ VEGETATION: _____ DEPTH:_____
LURE / BAIT TYPE: _____

COLOR: _____ SIZE: _____ MODEL: _____

ROD: _____ REEL:_____ LINE: _____

NOTES: _____

_____

═══

SPECIES:_____ LENGTH:_____ WEIGHT:_____

TIME CAUGHT:_____ LOCATION:_____

STUCTURE/ VEGETATION: _____ DEPTH:_____
LURE / BAIT TYPE: _____

COLOR: _____ SIZE: _____ MODEL: _____

ROD: _____ REEL:_____ LINE: _____

NOTES: _____

_____

SPECIES:_____ LENGTH: _____ WEIGHT: _____

TIME CAUGHT:_____ LOCATION:_____

STUCTURE/ VEGETATION: _____ DEPTH: _____
LURE / BAIT TYPE: _____

COLOR: _____ SIZE: _____ MODEL: _____

ROD: _____ REEL:_____ LINE: _____

NOTES: _____
_____

SPECIES:_____ LENGTH: _____ WEIGHT: _____

TIME CAUGHT:_____ LOCATION:_____

STUCTURE/ VEGETATION: _____ DEPTH: _____
LURE / BAIT TYPE: _____

COLOR: _____ SIZE: _____ MODEL: _____

ROD: _____ REEL:_____ LINE: _____

NOTES: _____
_____

SPECIES:_____ LENGTH: _____ WEIGHT: _____

TIME CAUGHT:_____ LOCATION:_____

STUCTURE/ VEGETATION: _____ DEPTH: _____
LURE / BAIT TYPE: _____

COLOR: _____ SIZE: _____ MODEL: _____

ROD: _____ REEL:_____ LINE: _____

NOTES: _____
_____

FISHING JOURNAL AND LOG BOOK

SPECIES BEING PURSUED _____

DATE: _____   TIME: _____   TO: _____

WHO I FISHED WITH: _____

WATER LOCATION DETAILS

BODY OF WATER: _____   LAUNCH RAMP: _____

WATER TEMP AT LAUNCH: _____   UPON RETURN : _____

WATER CLARITY:
☐ CLEAR ☐ STAINED ☐ MURKY ☐ MUDDY ☐ OTHER: _____

WATER LEVEL:
☐ NORMAL ☐ LOW ☐ HIGH ☐ DROPPING ☐ RISING

OTHER FACTORS:
☐ INSECT HATCHES ☐ BAIT FISH ☐ OTHER_____

WEATHER DETAILS

CURRENT AIR TEMP: _____   HIGH/LOW: _____ / _____

WIND SPEED: _____   DIRECTION: _____

MOON PHASE: _____   BAROMETER: _____

SUNRISE: _____   SUNSET: _____

CONDITIONS NOTED:
☐ SUNNY ☐ PARTLY CLOUDY ☐ CLOUDY ☐ STORM CLOUDS
☐ RAINING ☐ FOG ☐ DRIZZLE ☐ SLEET ☐ SNOW
☐ OTHER: _____

NOTES: _____

_____

_____

SPECIES:_____ LENGTH:_____ WEIGHT:_____

TIME CAUGHT:_____ LOCATION:_____

STUCTURE/ VEGETATION: _____ DEPTH:_____
LURE / BAIT TYPE: _____

COLOR: _____ SIZE: _____ MODEL: _____

ROD: _____ REEL:_____ LINE: _____

NOTES: _____
_____

SPECIES:_____ LENGTH:_____ WEIGHT:_____

TIME CAUGHT:_____ LOCATION:_____

STUCTURE/ VEGETATION: _____ DEPTH:_____
LURE / BAIT TYPE: _____

COLOR: _____ SIZE: _____ MODEL: _____

ROD: _____ REEL:_____ LINE: _____

NOTES: _____
_____

SPECIES:_____ LENGTH:_____ WEIGHT:_____

TIME CAUGHT:_____ LOCATION:_____

STUCTURE/ VEGETATION: _____ DEPTH:_____
LURE / BAIT TYPE: _____

COLOR: _____ SIZE: _____ MODEL: _____

ROD: _____ REEL:_____ LINE: _____

NOTES: _____
_____

SPECIES:_____ LENGTH:_____ WEIGHT:_____

TIME CAUGHT:_____ LOCATION:_____

STUCTURE/ VEGETATION: _____ DEPTH:_____
LURE / BAIT TYPE:
_____

COLOR: _____ SIZE: _____ MODEL: _____

ROD: _____ REEL:_____ LINE:_____

NOTES: _____

_____

SPECIES:_____ LENGTH:_____ WEIGHT:_____

TIME CAUGHT:_____ LOCATION:_____

STUCTURE/ VEGETATION: _____ DEPTH:_____
LURE / BAIT TYPE:
_____

COLOR: _____ SIZE: _____ MODEL: _____

ROD: _____ REEL:_____ LINE:_____

NOTES: _____

_____

SPECIES:_____ LENGTH:_____ WEIGHT:_____

TIME CAUGHT:_____ LOCATION:_____

STUCTURE/ VEGETATION: _____ DEPTH:_____
LURE / BAIT TYPE:
_____

COLOR: _____ SIZE: _____ MODEL: _____

ROD: _____ REEL:_____ LINE:_____

NOTES: _____

_____

SPECIES:_____ LENGTH: _____ WEIGHT: _____

TIME CAUGHT:_____ LOCATION:_____

STUCTURE/ VEGETATION: _____ DEPTH: _____
LURE / BAIT TYPE: _____

COLOR: _____ SIZE: _____ MODEL: _____

ROD: _____ REEL:_____ LINE: _____

NOTES: _____
_____

SPECIES:_____ LENGTH: _____ WEIGHT: _____

TIME CAUGHT:_____ LOCATION:_____

STUCTURE/ VEGETATION: _____ DEPTH: _____
LURE / BAIT TYPE: _____

COLOR: _____ SIZE: _____ MODEL: _____

ROD: _____ REEL:_____ LINE: _____

NOTES: _____
_____

SPECIES:_____ LENGTH: _____ WEIGHT: _____

TIME CAUGHT:_____ LOCATION:_____

STUCTURE/ VEGETATION: _____ DEPTH: _____
LURE / BAIT TYPE: _____

COLOR: _____ SIZE: _____ MODEL: _____

ROD: _____ REEL:_____ LINE: _____

NOTES: _____
_____

SPECIES:_____ LENGTH:_____ WEIGHT: _____

TIME CAUGHT:_____ LOCATION:_____

STUCTURE/ VEGETATION: _____ DEPTH: _____
LURE / BAIT TYPE: _____

COLOR: _____ SIZE: _____ MODEL: _____

ROD: _____ REEL:_____ LINE: _____

NOTES: _____
_____

═══

SPECIES:_____ LENGTH:_____ WEIGHT: _____

TIME CAUGHT:_____ LOCATION:_____

STUCTURE/ VEGETATION: _____ DEPTH: _____
LURE / BAIT TYPE: _____

COLOR: _____ SIZE: _____ MODEL: _____

ROD: _____ REEL:_____ LINE: _____

NOTES: _____
_____

═══

SPECIES:_____ LENGTH:_____ WEIGHT: _____

TIME CAUGHT:_____ LOCATION:_____

STUCTURE/ VEGETATION: _____ DEPTH: _____
LURE / BAIT TYPE: _____

COLOR: _____ SIZE: _____ MODEL: _____

ROD: _____ REEL:_____ LINE: _____

NOTES: _____
_____

FISHING JOURNAL AND LOG BOOK

SPECIES BEING PURSUED _____

DATE: _____   TIME: _____   TO: _____

WHO I FISHED WITH: _____

WATER LOCATION DETAILS

BODY OF WATER: _____   LAUNCH RAMP: _____

WATER TEMP AT LAUNCH: _____   UPON RETURN : _____

WATER CLARITY:
☐ CLEAR   ☐ STAINED   ☐ MURKY   ☐ MUDDY   ☐ OTHER: _____

WATER LEVEL:
☐ NORMAL   ☐ LOW   ☐ HIGH   ☐ DROPPING   ☐ RISING

OTHER FACTORS:
☐ INSECT HATCHES   ☐ BAIT FISH   ☐ OTHER_____

WEATHER DETAILS

CURRENT AIR TEMP: _____   HIGH/LOW:_____ / _____

WIND SPEED: _____   DIRECTION: _____

MOON PHASE: _____   BAROMETER:_____

SUNRISE: _____   SUNSET:_____

CONDITIONS NOTED:
☐ SUNNY   ☐ PARTLY CLOUDY   ☐ CLOUDY   ☐ STORM CLOUDS
☐ RAINING   ☐ FOG   ☐ DRIZZLE   ☐ SLEET   ☐ SNOW
☐ OTHER: _____

NOTES: _____

_____

_____

SPECIES:_____ LENGTH:_____ WEIGHT: _____

TIME CAUGHT:_____ LOCATION:_____

STUCTURE/ VEGETATION: _____ DEPTH: _____
LURE / BAIT TYPE: _____

COLOR: _____ SIZE: _____ MODEL: _____

ROD: _____ REEL:_____ LINE: _____

NOTES: _____
_____

SPECIES:_____ LENGTH:_____ WEIGHT: _____

TIME CAUGHT:_____ LOCATION:_____

STUCTURE/ VEGETATION: _____ DEPTH: _____
LURE / BAIT TYPE: _____

COLOR: _____ SIZE: _____ MODEL: _____

ROD: _____ REEL:_____ LINE: _____

NOTES: _____
_____

SPECIES:_____ LENGTH:_____ WEIGHT: _____

TIME CAUGHT:_____ LOCATION:_____

STUCTURE/ VEGETATION: _____ DEPTH: _____
LURE / BAIT TYPE: _____

COLOR: _____ SIZE: _____ MODEL: _____

ROD: _____ REEL:_____ LINE: _____

NOTES: _____
_____

SPECIES:_____ LENGTH:_____ WEIGHT: _____

TIME CAUGHT:_____ LOCATION:_____

STUCTURE/ VEGETATION: _____ DEPTH: _____
LURE / BAIT TYPE: _____

COLOR: _____ SIZE: _____ MODEL: _____

ROD: _____ REEL:_____ LINE: _____

NOTES: _____
_____

━━━━━━━━━━━━━━━━━━━━━━━━━━━━━━━

SPECIES:_____ LENGTH:_____ WEIGHT: _____

TIME CAUGHT:_____ LOCATION:_____

STUCTURE/ VEGETATION: _____ DEPTH: _____
LURE / BAIT TYPE: _____

COLOR: _____ SIZE: _____ MODEL: _____

ROD: _____ REEL:_____ LINE: _____

NOTES: _____
_____

━━━━━━━━━━━━━━━━━━━━━━━━━━━━━━━

SPECIES:_____ LENGTH:_____ WEIGHT: _____

TIME CAUGHT:_____ LOCATION:_____

STUCTURE/ VEGETATION: _____ DEPTH: _____
LURE / BAIT TYPE: _____

COLOR: _____ SIZE: _____ MODEL: _____

ROD: _____ REEL:_____ LINE: _____

NOTES: _____
_____

SPECIES:_____ LENGTH:_____ WEIGHT:_____

TIME CAUGHT:_____ LOCATION:_____

STUCTURE/ VEGETATION: _____ DEPTH:_____
LURE / BAIT TYPE: _____

COLOR: _____ SIZE: _____ MODEL: _____

ROD: _____ REEL:_____ LINE: _____

NOTES: _____

_____

SPECIES:_____ LENGTH:_____ WEIGHT:_____

TIME CAUGHT:_____ LOCATION:_____

STUCTURE/ VEGETATION: _____ DEPTH:_____
LURE / BAIT TYPE: _____

COLOR: _____ SIZE: _____ MODEL: _____

ROD: _____ REEL:_____ LINE: _____

NOTES: _____

_____

SPECIES:_____ LENGTH:_____ WEIGHT:_____

TIME CAUGHT:_____ LOCATION:_____

STUCTURE/ VEGETATION: _____ DEPTH:_____
LURE / BAIT TYPE: _____

COLOR: _____ SIZE: _____ MODEL: _____

ROD: _____ REEL:_____ LINE: _____

NOTES: _____

_____

SPECIES:_____ LENGTH: _____ WEIGHT: _____

TIME CAUGHT:_____ LOCATION:_____

STUCTURE/ VEGETATION: _____ DEPTH: _____
LURE / BAIT TYPE: _____

COLOR: _____ SIZE: _____ MODEL: _____

ROD: _____ REEL:_____ LINE: _____

NOTES: _____
_____

═══════════════════════════════════════

SPECIES:_____ LENGTH: _____ WEIGHT: _____

TIME CAUGHT:_____ LOCATION:_____

STUCTURE/ VEGETATION: _____ DEPTH: _____
LURE / BAIT TYPE: _____

COLOR: _____ SIZE: _____ MODEL: _____

ROD: _____ REEL:_____ LINE: _____

NOTES: _____
_____

═══════════════════════════════════════

SPECIES:_____ LENGTH: _____ WEIGHT: _____

TIME CAUGHT:_____ LOCATION:_____

STUCTURE/ VEGETATION: _____ DEPTH: _____
LURE / BAIT TYPE: _____

COLOR: _____ SIZE: _____ MODEL: _____

ROD: _____ REEL:_____ LINE: _____

NOTES: _____
_____

FISHING JOURNAL AND LOG BOOK

SPECIES BEING PURSUED _____

DATE: _____ TIME: _____ TO: _____

WHO I FISHED WITH: _____

WATER LOCATION DETAILS

BODY OF WATER: _____ LAUNCH RAMP: _____

WATER TEMP AT LAUNCH: _____ UPON RETURN : _____

WATER CLARITY:
☐ CLEAR ☐ STAINED ☐ MURKY ☐ MUDDY ☐ OTHER: _____

WATER LEVEL:
☐ NORMAL ☐ LOW ☐ HIGH ☐ DROPPING ☐ RISING

OTHER FACTORS:
☐ INSECT HATCHES ☐ BAIT FISH ☐ OTHER_____

WEATHER DETAILS

CURRENT AIR TEMP: _____ HIGH/LOW: _____ / _____

WIND SPEED: _____ DIRECTION: _____

MOON PHASE: _____ BAROMETER: _____

SUNRISE: _____ SUNSET: _____

CONDITIONS NOTED:
☐ SUNNY ☐ PARTLY CLOUDY ☐ CLOUDY ☐ STORM CLOUDS
☐ RAINING ☐ FOG ☐ DRIZZLE ☐ SLEET ☐ SNOW
☐ OTHER: _____

NOTES: _____

_____

_____

SPECIES:_____ LENGTH:_____ WEIGHT: _____

TIME CAUGHT:_____ LOCATION:_____

STUCTURE/ VEGETATION: _____ DEPTH: _____
LURE / BAIT TYPE: _____

COLOR: _____ SIZE: _____ MODEL: _____

ROD: _____ REEL:_____ LINE: _____

NOTES: _____

_____

SPECIES:_____ LENGTH:_____ WEIGHT: _____

TIME CAUGHT:_____ LOCATION:_____

STUCTURE/ VEGETATION: _____ DEPTH: _____
LURE / BAIT TYPE: _____

COLOR: _____ SIZE: _____ MODEL: _____

ROD: _____ REEL:_____ LINE: _____

NOTES: _____

_____

SPECIES:_____ LENGTH:_____ WEIGHT: _____

TIME CAUGHT:_____ LOCATION:_____

STUCTURE/ VEGETATION: _____ DEPTH: _____
LURE / BAIT TYPE: _____

COLOR: _____ SIZE: _____ MODEL: _____

ROD: _____ REEL:_____ LINE: _____

NOTES: _____

_____

SPECIES:_____ LENGTH: _____ WEIGHT: _____

TIME CAUGHT:_____ LOCATION:_____

STUCTURE/ VEGETATION: _____ DEPTH: _____
LURE / BAIT TYPE: _____

COLOR: _____ SIZE: _____ MODEL: _____

ROD: _____ REEL:_____ LINE: _____

NOTES: _____
_____

SPECIES:_____ LENGTH: _____ WEIGHT: _____

TIME CAUGHT:_____ LOCATION:_____

STUCTURE/ VEGETATION: _____ DEPTH: _____
LURE / BAIT TYPE: _____

COLOR: _____ SIZE: _____ MODEL: _____

ROD: _____ REEL:_____ LINE:_____

NOTES: _____
_____

SPECIES:_____ LENGTH: _____ WEIGHT: _____

TIME CAUGHT:_____ LOCATION:_____

STUCTURE/ VEGETATION: _____ DEPTH: _____
LURE / BAIT TYPE: _____

COLOR: _____ SIZE: _____ MODEL: _____

ROD: _____ REEL:_____ LINE: _____

NOTES: _____
_____

SPECIES:_____ LENGTH:_____ WEIGHT: _____

TIME CAUGHT:_____ LOCATION:_____

STUCTURE/ VEGETATION: _____ DEPTH: _____
LURE / BAIT TYPE: _____

COLOR: _____ SIZE: _____ MODEL: _____

ROD: _____ REEL:_____ LINE: _____

NOTES: _____
_____

SPECIES:_____ LENGTH:_____ WEIGHT: _____

TIME CAUGHT:_____ LOCATION:_____

STUCTURE/ VEGETATION: _____ DEPTH: _____
LURE / BAIT TYPE: _____

COLOR: _____ SIZE: _____ MODEL: _____

ROD: _____ REEL:_____ LINE: _____

NOTES: _____
_____

SPECIES:_____ LENGTH:_____ WEIGHT: _____

TIME CAUGHT:_____ LOCATION:_____

STUCTURE/ VEGETATION: _____ DEPTH: _____
LURE / BAIT TYPE: _____

COLOR: _____ SIZE: _____ MODEL: _____

ROD: _____ REEL:_____ LINE: _____

NOTES: _____
_____

SPECIES:_____ LENGTH:_____ WEIGHT: _____

TIME CAUGHT:_____ LOCATION:_____

STUCTURE/ VEGETATION: _____ DEPTH: _____
LURE / BAIT TYPE: _____

COLOR: _____ SIZE: _____ MODEL: _____

ROD: _____ REEL:_____ LINE: _____

NOTES: _____
_____

SPECIES:_____ LENGTH:_____ WEIGHT: _____

TIME CAUGHT:_____ LOCATION:_____

STUCTURE/ VEGETATION: _____ DEPTH: _____
LURE / BAIT TYPE: _____

COLOR: _____ SIZE: _____ MODEL: _____

ROD: _____ REEL:_____ LINE: _____

NOTES: _____
_____

SPECIES:_____ LENGTH:_____ WEIGHT: _____

TIME CAUGHT:_____ LOCATION:_____

STUCTURE/ VEGETATION: _____ DEPTH: _____
LURE / BAIT TYPE: _____

COLOR: _____ SIZE: _____ MODEL: _____

ROD: _____ REEL:_____ LINE: _____

NOTES: _____
_____

FISHING JOURNAL AND LOG BOOK

SPECIES BEING PURSUED _____

DATE: _____ TIME: _____ TO: _____

WHO I FISHED WITH: _____

WATER LOCATION DETAILS
BODY OF WATER: _____ LAUNCH RAMP: _____

WATER TEMP AT LAUNCH: _____ UPON RETURN : _____

WATER CLARITY:
☐ CLEAR ☐ STAINED ☐ MURKY ☐ MUDDY ☐ OTHER: _____

WATER LEVEL:
☐ NORMAL ☐ LOW ☐ HIGH ☐ DROPPING ☐ RISING

OTHER FACTORS:
☐ INSECT HATCHES ☐ BAIT FISH ☐ OTHER_____

WEATHER DETAILS
CURRENT AIR TEMP: _____ HIGH/LOW: _____ / _____

WIND SPEED: _____ DIRECTION: _____

MOON PHASE: _____ BAROMETER: _____

SUNRISE: _____ SUNSET: _____

CONDITIONS NOTED:
☐ SUNNY ☐ PARTLY CLOUDY ☐ CLOUDY ☐ STORM CLOUDS
☐ RAINING ☐ FOG ☐ DRIZZLE ☐ SLEET ☐ SNOW
☐ OTHER: _____

NOTES: _____

_____

_____

SPECIES:_____ LENGTH:_____ WEIGHT:_____

TIME CAUGHT:_____ LOCATION:_____

STUCTURE/ VEGETATION: _____ DEPTH:_____
LURE / BAIT TYPE: _____

COLOR: _____ SIZE: _____ MODEL: _____

ROD: _____ REEL:_____ LINE: _____

NOTES: _____

_____

SPECIES:_____ LENGTH:_____ WEIGHT:_____

TIME CAUGHT:_____ LOCATION:_____

STUCTURE/ VEGETATION: _____ DEPTH:_____
LURE / BAIT TYPE: _____

COLOR: _____ SIZE: _____ MODEL: _____

ROD: _____ REEL:_____ LINE: _____

NOTES: _____

_____

SPECIES:_____ LENGTH:_____ WEIGHT:_____

TIME CAUGHT:_____ LOCATION:_____

STUCTURE/ VEGETATION: _____ DEPTH:_____
LURE / BAIT TYPE: _____

COLOR: _____ SIZE: _____ MODEL: _____

ROD: _____ REEL:_____ LINE: _____

NOTES: _____

_____

SPECIES:_____ LENGTH:_____ WEIGHT:_____

TIME CAUGHT:_____ LOCATION:_____

STUCTURE/ VEGETATION: _____ DEPTH:_____
LURE / BAIT TYPE:
_____

COLOR: _____ SIZE: _____ MODEL: _____

ROD: _____ REEL:_____ LINE: _____

NOTES: _____

_____

SPECIES:_____ LENGTH:_____ WEIGHT:_____

TIME CAUGHT:_____ LOCATION:_____

STUCTURE/ VEGETATION: _____ DEPTH:_____
LURE / BAIT TYPE:
_____

COLOR: _____ SIZE: _____ MODEL: _____

ROD: _____ REEL:_____ LINE: _____

NOTES: _____

_____

SPECIES:_____ LENGTH:_____ WEIGHT:_____

TIME CAUGHT:_____ LOCATION:_____

STUCTURE/ VEGETATION: _____ DEPTH:_____
LURE / BAIT TYPE:
_____

COLOR: _____ SIZE: _____ MODEL: _____

ROD: _____ REEL:_____ LINE: _____

NOTES: _____

_____

SPECIES:_____ LENGTH:_____ WEIGHT:_____

TIME CAUGHT:_____ LOCATION:_____

STUCTURE/ VEGETATION: _____ DEPTH:_____
LURE / BAIT TYPE: _____

COLOR: _____ SIZE: _____ MODEL: _____

ROD: _____ REEL:_____ LINE: _____

NOTES: _____

_____

===================================

SPECIES:_____ LENGTH:_____ WEIGHT:_____

TIME CAUGHT:_____ LOCATION:_____

STUCTURE/ VEGETATION: _____ DEPTH:_____
LURE / BAIT TYPE: _____

COLOR: _____ SIZE: _____ MODEL: _____

ROD: _____ REEL:_____ LINE: _____

NOTES: _____

_____

===================================

SPECIES:_____ LENGTH:_____ WEIGHT:_____

TIME CAUGHT:_____ LOCATION:_____

STUCTURE/ VEGETATION: _____ DEPTH:_____
LURE / BAIT TYPE: _____

COLOR: _____ SIZE: _____ MODEL: _____

ROD: _____ REEL:_____ LINE: _____

NOTES: _____

_____

SPECIES:_____ LENGTH: _____ WEIGHT: _____

TIME CAUGHT:_____ LOCATION:_____

STUCTURE/ VEGETATION: _____ DEPTH: _____
LURE / BAIT TYPE: _____

COLOR: _____ SIZE: _____ MODEL: _____

ROD: _____ REEL:_____ LINE: _____

NOTES: _____
_____

═══════════════════════════════════════

SPECIES:_____ LENGTH: _____ WEIGHT: _____

TIME CAUGHT:_____ LOCATION:_____

STUCTURE/ VEGETATION: _____ DEPTH: _____
LURE / BAIT TYPE: _____

COLOR: _____ SIZE: _____ MODEL: _____

ROD: _____ REEL:_____ LINE: _____

NOTES: _____
_____

═══════════════════════════════════════

SPECIES:_____ LENGTH: _____ WEIGHT: _____

TIME CAUGHT:_____ LOCATION:_____

STUCTURE/ VEGETATION: _____ DEPTH: _____
LURE / BAIT TYPE: _____

COLOR: _____ SIZE: _____ MODEL: _____

ROD: _____ REEL:_____ LINE: _____

NOTES: _____

FISHING JOURNAL AND LOG BOOK

SPECIES BEING PURSUED _____

DATE: _____   TIME: _____   TO: _____

WHO I FISHED WITH: _____

WATER LOCATION DETAILS

BODY OF WATER: _____   LAUNCH RAMP: _____

WATER TEMP AT LAUNCH: _____   UPON RETURN : _____

WATER CLARITY:
☐ CLEAR ☐ STAINED ☐ MURKY ☐ MUDDY ☐ OTHER: _____

WATER LEVEL:
☐ NORMAL ☐ LOW ☐ HIGH ☐ DROPPING ☐ RISING

OTHER FACTORS:
☐ INSECT HATCHES ☐ BAIT FISH ☐ OTHER_____

WEATHER DETAILS

CURRENT AIR TEMP: _____   HIGH/LOW: _____ / _____

WIND SPEED: _____   DIRECTION: _____

MOON PHASE: _____   BAROMETER: _____

SUNRISE: _____   SUNSET: _____

CONDITIONS NOTED:
☐ SUNNY ☐ PARTLY CLOUDY ☐ CLOUDY ☐ STORM CLOUDS
☐ RAINING ☐ FOG ☐ DRIZZLE ☐ SLEET ☐ SNOW
☐ OTHER: _____

NOTES: _____

_____

_____

SPECIES:_____ LENGTH:_____ WEIGHT: _____

TIME CAUGHT:_____ LOCATION:_____

STUCTURE/ VEGETATION: _____ DEPTH:_____
LURE / BAIT TYPE: _____

COLOR: _____ SIZE: _____ MODEL: _____

ROD: _____ REEL:_____ LINE: _____

NOTES: _____

_____

SPECIES:_____ LENGTH:_____ WEIGHT: _____

TIME CAUGHT:_____ LOCATION:_____

STUCTURE/ VEGETATION: _____ DEPTH:_____
LURE / BAIT TYPE: _____

COLOR: _____ SIZE: _____ MODEL: _____

ROD: _____ REEL:_____ LINE: _____

NOTES: _____

_____

SPECIES:_____ LENGTH:_____ WEIGHT: _____

TIME CAUGHT:_____ LOCATION:_____

STUCTURE/ VEGETATION: _____ DEPTH:_____
LURE / BAIT TYPE: _____

COLOR: _____ SIZE: _____ MODEL: _____

ROD: _____ REEL:_____ LINE: _____

NOTES: _____

_____

SPECIES:_____ LENGTH:_____ WEIGHT:_____

TIME CAUGHT:_____ LOCATION:_____

STUCTURE/ VEGETATION: _____ DEPTH:_____
LURE / BAIT TYPE: _____

COLOR: _____ SIZE: _____ MODEL: _____

ROD: _____ REEL:_____ LINE:_____

NOTES: _____

_____

═══

SPECIES:_____ LENGTH:_____ WEIGHT:_____

TIME CAUGHT:_____ LOCATION:_____

STUCTURE/ VEGETATION: _____ DEPTH:_____
LURE / BAIT TYPE: _____

COLOR: _____ SIZE: _____ MODEL: _____

ROD: _____ REEL:_____ LINE:_____

NOTES: _____

_____

═══

SPECIES:_____ LENGTH:_____ WEIGHT:_____

TIME CAUGHT:_____ LOCATION:_____

STUCTURE/ VEGETATION: _____ DEPTH:_____
LURE / BAIT TYPE: _____

COLOR: _____ SIZE: _____ MODEL: _____

ROD: _____ REEL:_____ LINE:_____

NOTES: _____

_____

SPECIES:_____ LENGTH:_____ WEIGHT: _____

TIME CAUGHT:_____ LOCATION:_____

STUCTURE/ VEGETATION: _____ DEPTH: _____
LURE / BAIT TYPE: _____

COLOR: _____ SIZE: _____ MODEL: _____

ROD: _____ REEL:_____ LINE: _____

NOTES: _____

_____

SPECIES:_____ LENGTH:_____ WEIGHT: _____

TIME CAUGHT:_____ LOCATION:_____

STUCTURE/ VEGETATION: _____ DEPTH: _____
LURE / BAIT TYPE: _____

COLOR: _____ SIZE: _____ MODEL: _____

ROD: _____ REEL:_____ LINE: _____

NOTES: _____

_____

SPECIES:_____ LENGTH:_____ WEIGHT: _____

TIME CAUGHT:_____ LOCATION:_____

STUCTURE/ VEGETATION: _____ DEPTH: _____
LURE / BAIT TYPE: _____

COLOR: _____ SIZE: _____ MODEL: _____

ROD: _____ REEL:_____ LINE: _____

NOTES: _____

_____

SPECIES:_____ LENGTH: _____ WEIGHT: _____

TIME CAUGHT:_____ LOCATION:_____

STUCTURE/ VEGETATION: _____ DEPTH: _____
LURE / BAIT TYPE: _____

COLOR: _____ SIZE: _____ MODEL: _____

ROD: _____ REEL:_____ LINE: _____

NOTES: _____
_____

═══

SPECIES:_____ LENGTH: _____ WEIGHT: _____

TIME CAUGHT:_____ LOCATION:_____

STUCTURE/ VEGETATION: _____ DEPTH: _____
LURE / BAIT TYPE: _____

COLOR: _____ SIZE: _____ MODEL: _____

ROD: _____ REEL:_____ LINE: _____

NOTES: _____
_____

═══

SPECIES:_____ LENGTH: _____ WEIGHT: _____

TIME CAUGHT:_____ LOCATION:_____

STUCTURE/ VEGETATION: _____ DEPTH: _____
LURE / BAIT TYPE: _____

COLOR: _____ SIZE: _____ MODEL: _____

ROD: _____ REEL:_____ LINE: _____

NOTES: _____
_____

Manufactured by Amazon.ca
Bolton, ON

15633363R00069